1978.

What Methodists Believe

RUPERT E. DAVIES

MOWBRAYS
LONDON & OXFORD

© A. R. Mowbray 1976
Text set in Linotype Baskerville
and printed and bound in Great Britain by
Richard Clay (The Chaucer Press), Ltd.,
Bungay, Suffolk

ISBN 0 264 66340 3

First published 1976 by
A. R. Mowbray & Co. Ltd.
The Alden Press, Osney Mead, Oxford OX2 0EG

Contents

Preface

ANYONE picking up a book with the title which this one bears might well expect to find a full account of the beliefs which Methodist Christians hold, but other Christians may or may not, with a brief reference at the beginning or the end to the beliefs which Methodists hold in common with other Christians. But I could not write such a book, for I am completely convinced that the common beliefs of all Christians are far more numerous and important than those which are peculiar to Methodists, and to lay especial emphasis on Methodist beliefs would, for me, garble the truth and put the whole book off balance. I am certain that a large part of the answer to the question, 'What do Methodists believe?' consists in saying what all Christians believe.

But I am equally convinced that Methodism has distinctive features of great importance for all Christians, and these I have attempted to describe. The tradition within Christianity which John Wesley took over and brought back to life, and offered unsuccessfully to the Anglicanism of his time, is alive and strong, and gives a special flavour to the way in which Methodists live, believe and think.

As in other Churches, there are schools of thought within Methodism. We have our 'conservatives', some extreme and some not; we have our radicals; we have our 'High Churchmen', we have our militant Protestants. But most of us are in the centre or near it, and I hope that what I have written represents the standpoint of a central Methodism which is ready to learn from all the schools of thought.

I owe a very great deal to my wife and family, all of them critical Methodists, asking awkward questions with some frequency; to my former and present colleagues in the Methodist ministry and laity; to Mrs Mary Tanner, who, as an ecumenical Anglican theologian, has tried to save me both from saying things which only a Methodist can understand, and from falling into the danger, always involved in writing a short book on great subjects, of over-simplifying and falsifying complex issues; and to Mrs Ann Weeks, a member of my present congregation, who has achieved, without turning a hair, the mammoth task of deciphering my handwriting and transforming it into typescript.

RUPERT E. DAVIES

Nailsea, Bristol, February 1976

Foreword

RUPERT DAVIES has a rare combination of talents. He is a noted Methodist scholar with a gift for popular exposition. Through his influence on the important Faith and Order Committee, he has done much to help shape Methodist worship and church-manship. He has been President of the Methodist Conference, taught generations of students for the Ministry and now his career has turned full-circle —he is that species of minister whom Wesley re-garded as central to the proper ordering and effi-ciency of Methodism—a circuit Superintendent. So at the very least, the judgements in this book can be relied upon because they are the result of a fusion between sound scholarship and versatile experience at every level of Methodism.

Personally, I am delighted that Mr Davies has taken as his starting point the common Christian heritage. Methodism, as he knows better than I, functions best within an encompassing environment of catholicity, in the strict sense of the term—the universal Christian community. It was not Wesley's intention that we should go it alone; on the other hand, he would have no truck with any wheeling-dealing which involved achieving spurious unity at the expense of evident truth. So this is the account of a Church *ad interim* forever seeking to fulfil its destiny as an order of evangelism, discipline, worship and nurture within what Wesley called 'The Great Congregation of the Baptised'.

20th century Methodism is undergoing a crisis of identity. As Mr Davies points out, the powerful missionary impetus has helped to nurture, under God, churches of the Methodist ilk throughout the world, some with bishops, some without—one indeed, is headed by a Patriarch. All have been stamped with the hall-mark of authentic Wesley influence, but because each is incarnate within, and has to respond to, diverse cultural conditions, World Methodism is easier to define statistically as one of the biggest Protestant Communions than to describe in credal terms.

Such a book as this—brief, popular but accurate—cried out to be written, as much so that modern Methodists might rediscover who they are and where they stand, as that others can indulge their legitimate curiosity about the 'People called Methodists' and hopefully catch a glimpse of the vision which fired John Wesley, with such momentous consequences for the renewal of the Church and the transformation of society.

I am personally grateful to Rupert Davies for many kindnesses, but for none more than this book, which gives me cause for a certain amount of judicious pride, if that is permissible in an ecumenical age, for all that Methodism is and has done for me.

COLIN M. MORRIS,
President of the Methodist Conference
July 1976.

Introduction: Questions That Must be Asked

'ASK NO questions, and you'll be told no lies', children used to be informed. The trouble is that if you ask no questions, you will not be told the *truth* either. Anyway, no sensible human being takes life just as it comes, without asking questions about it, even if the right answers do not come first time. Asking questions is an important part of being human. So we'll take as a motto for this book the old rhyme:

> I have six honest serving men who taught me
>   all I knew;
> Their names are 'what' and 'how' and 'when'
>   and 'where' and 'why' and 'who'.
> I send them abroad on my own affairs, from
>   the moment I open my eyes:
> Two million hows, three million wheres and
>   seven million whys.

Of course, the snag about asking so many questions is that they cannot all be answered—or cannot be answered in a way which satisfies everyone. Some of them, fortunately, have a definite and satisfactory answer. Others have an answer which satisfies people in one age, but has to be looked at again and may be changed by a succeeding age. And some are still completely baffling; we just have to continue work-ing on them until someone, in this or a later genera-tion, comes up with the answer. And some of these may never receive an answer at all.

These questions that we all ask can be conveni-ently divided into three classes. The first group concerns practical everyday living—the 'bread and butter' questions, although they are not all about food. Many of them are the sort of questions you'll find in a guide book to a foreign country, translated for you into the language of the country—the things you need to know for definite practical purposes. 'Where can I buy some bread?' 'How far is it to the station?' 'Which is the best way to the chemist?' 'How much does it cost to buy a bicycle?' And then in a different department of life: 'How many O-levels do I need to apply for the job?' 'How many A-levels does such and such a university require?' etc., etc., etc. The point about these questions is that the answer is simply factual, and usually easy to find. And when it is found, there is no argument about it (or need not be).

The second type is made up of the scientific, historical, linguistic and literary questions which provide the material for the greater part of the school curriculum. The scientific ones are about the constituent elements in the liquids and solids and gases which make up the earth and the things and animals on it, and the ways in which these liquids, solids and gases are known to behave on their own and in relation to each other. The historical ones are about the events of the past, and their causes and results, leading on to problems about the motives, characters and policies of those who were in some way responsible for them. The linguistic questions are about the right way to express ideas in our own and other languages, and to translate ideas from one language to another. The literary ones are about such things as who wrote which poem to whom, and when, why and where did he write it, and what was the meaning and value of it when it was written and what significance and value does it have now?

The advance of civilisation depends on the accumulation of answers to these questions, and the last two hundred years have witnessed an immense increase in our knowledge about the scientific ones, that is, about the physical, chemical and biological constitution of the world and its inhabitants. But new questions are always arising, and some of the older questions are not yet answered, or are answered in different ways by different experts. For instance, there are two theories about the nature of light, both of which may well be true, but are not easy to reconcile with each other. The nature of life itself is still under scrutiny; it is difficult to say exactly what it is, or how to produce it. Nuclear science has posed a whole host of new questions in the last fifty years, while well-established theories about matter or the human mind sometimes come under severe criticism in a later generation.

Historical and literary questions are rarely answered so conclusively as scientific questions, though certain agreed answers do gradually emerge. We can be fairly certain that Julius Caesar was murdered on 15 March 44 B.C., and some at least of the reasons for his murder are known. The same applies to the Battle of Waterloo, and many other past events. Many of the events of the Second World War are still in dispute, both as to what happened and why it happened, but the elements of truth and error in the various accounts are slowly being sorted out. Literary questions will be debated until the end of time, because they are so much matters of personal judgement. Yet, in spite of this, there is general agreement that the Bible, Shakespeare, Goethe and a few others are superior in most ways to the common run of literature, and should be studied by each succeeding generation. So when we tackle these numerous and varied questions we enter a country with expanding frontiers, for as knowledge increases the area of inquiry is constantly enlarged. And even on subjects where there are large resources of agreed knowledge, there is often much that is still in dispute between people with different theories and ways of life.

It is certainly absurd to say 'Science teaches that ...' or 'History teaches that ...'; as soon as you say what science or history is supposed to teach, an uproar breaks out among the scientists or historians present. Yet an immense amount of truth, scientific, historical and literary has been discovered, and the process will go steadily on. The human race can look back on its achievements in this regard with legitimate pride, so long as it does not claim to have exhausted its search for knowledge, or to be about to do so, and so long as it does not forget that the more we know, the more we realise there is to know.

The third class of question is the most important and the most difficult of all. It is made up of questions that human beings have been asking since they started to see that the immediate needs of everyday life raised questions that went beyond those immediate needs; and they are still being asked. Answers to some of them have emerged after centuries of reflection by the greatest minds which the human

12

race has produced. Most of these questions and the answers given are still disputed, or presented in all sorts of different ways. And some of them have as yet received no convincing answers.

These are the ultimate questions, the questions that commonsense, science, history and literature cannot answer by using their own methods alone. Here are some of them: Is there any point or purpose in human life? Human beings are born, grow up, fall ill, recover, grow old and die. Between birth and death they experience both pleasure and pain in differing proportions; they eat and drink and think and talk and feel and desire and fear and hope, they have relationships with each other, some close, some distant, some long lasting, some brief. And at the end what does it all amount to? Is any purpose served, any meaning shown?

> Solomon Grundy,
> Born on Monday,
> Christened on Tuesday,
> Married on Wednesday,
> Fell ill on Thursday,
> Worse on Friday,
> Died on Saturday,
> Buried on Sunday,
> And that was the end of Solomon Grundy.

Is that all there is to it? Or is there some meaning to it which goes beyond the mere succession of events and the individual to whom they happen, something which makes it worthwhile to work hard and live as well as possible?

'Live as well as possible.' That brings us to a second question. What does it mean to 'live as well as possible'? That seems to imply that there is a difference between living well and living badly, some difference between good and evil, right and wrong. But is there any such difference, and if there is, does it matter? Parents and teachers and parsons are constantly harping on 'doing what is right', but is 'right' anything more than what these same parents, teachers and parsons find convenient to themselves if other people do it? If everyone tells the truth and people help each other, life is much easier for older people in positions of authority. So, of course, they encourage their juniors to tell the truth and help each other. They may even actually believe that in some mysterious way truth-telling is superior to lying, and unselfishness, but are they right? Haven't they just been conditioned to that way of thinking when they were young?

Now these same older people sometimes say that 'right' is 'what God wants to happen'. But that brings us to a third question: is there a God? Isn't God just an idea in the human mind? When the world was even more strange and dangerous than it is, didn't people think up God as a useful explanation of everything and as someone whom they could ask to look after them? Now we don't need this idea any more, as we know why things happen —or soon will—and we know that we have to look after ourselves in the universe anyway. What are the arguments, if any, for believing that God really exists?

It's obvious that God, even if he exists, can't be seen or heard in the normal way. There's something else, too, which can't be seen or heard in the normal way, but in which many people believe. This is life after death. When people die, they are buried or

cremated, and the remains go to form other sub-
stances in or on the earth. That surely means that
when they're dead, they're done for. Yet people all
over the world and in all periods of history persist
in believing that they will live on after death. Is
this just wishful thinking, or is there some good
reason for believing this? It's very important to
know the answer to this, as it will affect the way in
which we live now, but we hear nothing but differing views. So this is a fourth question: is there a life
after death—and if so, what sort of life is it?

It's the aim of this book to look at the sort of questions that we have called 'ultimate', and to explain
how Christians answer them. We have seen that they
are questions to which no answer can be found in
ordinary living or by simply studying the ordinary
subjects on the school time-table. Only by going as
deeply as possible into the deepest thoughts of the
deepest thinkers and forming our own carefully
thought out view of the universe can we hope to get
anywhere.

Christian faith does not offer a set of cut-and-
dried answers to the great problems of the universe.
But it does suggest an approach to them. This approach is common to all kinds of Christian thinker,
though the detailed application of this approach
to individual questions differs sometimes from denomination to denomination, and inside the denominations themselves. What follows is mostly an
account of Christian agreement on essentials, with
indications of the points on which Methodists would
lay a special emphasis that other Christians would
not necessarily share.

PART I

THE GROUND ALL CHRISTIANS HAVE IN COMMON

I

Jesus Christ Makes Sense of Man and God

JESUS CHRIST is the centre and mainspring of Christian faith. To say what Christians believe without putting him in the forefront of everything that is said would be like trying to play a game of cricket without having a batsman at the wicket.

Yet many people, many Christians even, have a very hazy idea of who Jesus Christ was, how he lived, and what he said and did. Perhaps in come cases their early teaching led them to imagine him as a sort of younger Father Christmas, or as a kindly dispenser of goodies from fairyland or Disneyland. If so, it is not surprising that when they grew up they stopped taking him seriously; he went into the back of their minds with the other favourites of their childish imaginations.

But he was a real person, and it is important to get quite straight the known facts about him. It is true that we do not know as much about him as we should like to know. The people who wrote the Gospels did not go about their work in the same way as a modern biographer or historian; nor had the things he said been taken down word for word by his hearers, or the things he did accurately observed and immediately described in writing by trained witnesses. There were no cine-cameras and no reporters in Galilee.

Yet we know enough to form a picture of his character, his career, his message and his activities. For in days when books were few and scarce, and many people in any case had not been taught how to read them, the human memory was a more capacious and retentive instrument than it needs to be nowadays. The important facts that a man wanted to know could not be looked up in a book or a magazine; he had to rely on his memory, or the memory of others. So he stored his memory with everything that he did not wish to lose; and when there were sayings or exploits that a group of people wished to remember, they met together frequently and repeated them again and again, as far as possible word for word. Even today many families have unwritten 'annals' of this kind. Every member of the family knows them off by heart, from having heard them so often, and woe betide the stranger who gets the story wrong!

The followers of Jesus believed what he had said and done to be the most important words and deeds in the whole history of mankind, and certainly in their own history. So they treasured them in their memories and repeated them endlessly. The Gospels give us what the early Church remembered, preached and taught about Jesus. Of course, as time went on, details may have fallen out, and others may have been added, for even the best memories do funny things; but they were as careful as they could possibly be.

The process of remembering and reminding each other went on for thirty or forty years before these recollections were written down once and for all in the Gospels; but, years before that, collections of sayings, parables and stories about Jesus were made and circulated. Although there are parts of the Gospels where we sometimes wonder if the writer has got the story quite right, the overall impression that we gain is that we have a consistent and reliable picture of Jesus in the Gospels and that they give us the true pattern of his teaching.

What, then, do we know? Jesus was a Jew, born during the reign of the Roman emperor Augustus, who had established a period of peace and prosperity throughout the countries which bordered the Mediterranean Sea. The country of Jesus' birth, Judaea, which included Bethlehem and Jerusalem, was a somewhat unimportant province of Augustus' empire, but which, because of the intense religious and political nationalism of its inhabitants, was liable to give more trouble to Rome than most other places. It was therefore placed under a military governor, with a strong garrison. To the North (with Samaria in between) was Galilee, where Jesus spent most of his life and carried out most of his work. This had been placed under native rulers from a line of half-Jews, the Herods, whom the Romans believed they could trust to keep the troublesome inhabitants in order. Jesus was a Jew, not only in race, but in religion. There was much in the Judaism of this time that was superficial and hypocritical, as Jesus himself was not slow to point out; but there were also profoundly genuine people with a real and living faith. This faith was centred in the living God who had redeemed his people, and was worshipped in the solemn sacrifices offered in the Temple in Jerusalem. Outside the capital the local synagogues focused the loyalty of ordinary people to the law of God and instructed them in the teaching of the prophets. Within the community of faithful Jews there were groups of teachers and disciples who emphasised certain aspects of the Law and carried them out with especial devotion; of these the Pharisees were a notable example. The Sadducees also professed great loyalty to the Law, but were suspected of collaborating too much with their Roman masters. Other groups formed separate communities, like the one in Qumran, near Jericho, where a particularly austere interpretation of the Law was practised.

Jesus in his youth attended the synagogue, applied himself assiduously to the study of the Law and the Prophets; and with his family made pilgrimages to Jerusalem to take part in the great festivals—as every devout Jew desired to do from time to time. He lived a quiet and ordinary life until he was about thirty. He never married.

The appearance and fiery eloquence of John the Baptist in the countryside not far from Nazareth was a decisive point in Jesus' life. John denounced the sins of his contemporaries, high and low, and called all and sundry to repentance, to be symbolised by total immersion in the river Jordan. He also foretold the imminent arrival of the long-awaited Messiah, the man from heaven anointed by God to bring deliverance to the Jewish people. Jesus joined him and was baptised. Soon afterwards the leader was arrested by the ruler of Galilee as a danger to public order; and Jesus took this as a signal for him to continue the mission of John.

But his message and his methods turned out more and more to be different from those of John. He had reflected for a long time on his own role within the purposes of God, and taken into account the many different ways in which Old Testament writers spoke of the one who would bring in God's rule on earth.

He had directly rejected the idea of setting up as a popular miracle-worker, and the temptation to gain as much power for himself as possible by the use of his outstanding gifts. He seems to have set his face against the widespread Jewish dream that a military leader would overthrow the power of Rome in the name of God, and to have been much more influenced by the notion that a successor to King David would set up a régime of peace and righteousness on earth, centred in Jerusalem. This is set out in the writings of Isaiah, the eighth-century prophet. He was inwardly impressed, too, by the idea to be found in the later books of the Old Testament, such as Daniel, and in other books not in the Old Testament, that God would suddenly intervene in human affairs by sending a superhuman personage to take over control. And we know that he identified himself with the faithful servant of God described in a set of poems imbedded in the writings of Isaiah, but written two centuries after Isaiah's lifetime (see chapters 49.1–6, and 53, for instance). This 'servant of God' was to give light to all the nations—and not to his own nation only; he was to follow his calling to the death, though 'tormented and humbled' by suffering, and he was to do and endure all this for the sake of all men, for 'we had all strayed like sheep, each of us had gone his own way; but the Lord laid on him the guilt of us all'.

Jesus developed this by seeing the servant's task as something which he must at all costs perform himself, in his own person, and at the same time as something which he must share with his friends. Later it was to be the responsibility laid upon the whole community which he was bringing into existence. He began his public career by declaring that the Kingdom of God had arrived; and he soon went on to say that it was present in his own person and in his own activities. That phrase, 'the Kingdom of God', has meant so many different and contradictory things at various times to various people that it is very hard to get back to the meaning which Jesus conveyed to his hearers. But we can be helped to understand it if we concentrate on the idea that the 'Kingdom of God' means the 'royal rule of God' —just that. God's rule, though never withdrawn by God himself, had been set aside by human injustice, cruelty, pride, selfishness. Now Jesus had reasserted it, and was summoning everyone to enter it by renewing their love for God and their obedience to him, and so bringing into operation within human affairs the justice, compassion, humility, unselfishness and love which God intended men to show towards each other. The situation like this in ordinary human life is when the ruler of a nation has been dethroned and exiled, but returns to his country, sets up his headquarters in a particular place and calls on all his countrymen to rally to the standard.

Jesus offered himself as the personal focus and embodiment of the Kingdom of God, and made good his claim to this position by doing for people what they knew only God could do. He forgave their sins, and restored them to health and wholeness. Since he was God's representative in person, he was able to say plainly that to become his followers was to enter the Kingdom of God; to reject him and his message was to reject God's rule.

In the process of re-establishing God's rule, he demonstrated the principles by which the lives of those who accepted that rule were to be governed. The Sermon on the Mount and many other utterances of Jesus have often been misunderstood. They were not set out by Jesus to be a blueprint for the improvement of human society as it is at present constituted; as such, they would be entirely impracticable and absurd. They are addressed to those who wish to obey the royal rule of God, and who look for his help in doing it. Nor do they give precise regulations for any human life or society whatever. God's loyal subjects are not asked to obey literally, in every situation, the command to give money to everyone who asks for it, or literally to turn the other cheek to every mugger or kidnapper who might attack them in New York, London or Calcutta. Jesus gave the two general principles on which life under the rule of God is based: love God with your whole self, and love your fellow human being as you love yourself. Then in stories and sayings, and by unfailing example, he showed how these general principles are to be worked out in the varying situations with which we are faced every day.

Jesus' 'Kingdom of God movement' got off to a spectacular start in his own neighbourhood and the surrounding countryside, especially as its most immediately visible results were the cures of disabled, seriously ill and mentally unstable people. But the crowds which flocked after Jesus scarcely understood at all the inner meaning of what he was doing and saying; and even his closest friends found it difficult to grasp. They did not see that it ran counter to many people's deeply cherished ideas, prejudices and plans. So he had to spend more and more time explaining that to follow him not only meant friendship and real happiness but also involved the serious and increasing possibility of persecution and death.

No one, not even his intimates, wanted to believe this at first, but as the opposition from the religious leaders of the country, both local and national, began to mount, the superficial followers of Jesus melted away, and his real followers began to brace themselves to go with him to death. Jesus set out on his career with the set purpose, not of being put to death, for this need not have happened if his teaching had been accepted by the nation's leaders, but of going through with his work as the servant of God, following the principles which the servant of God must follow, even if going through with it meant his own liquidation.

And this is what in fact it did mean. The priests and the teachers of the Law, perhaps with a few exceptions, were too concerned with maintaining their own interpretation of the Law, and with it their own position of pre-eminence, to listen to, let alone to accept, the teaching of Jesus about the love of God for all men, including scoundrels and dropouts. And the Roman military governor, not interested in religious subtleties, was greatly relieved to have the chance both of getting rid of someone who might have turned out to be a rebel, and of making himself temporarily popular with his awkward Jewish subjects all at one blow.

Jesus made no effort to oppose or resist the forces that were massing against him, though in order to face the prospect of a brutal death he had to summon all the inward resources which he believed that God could provide. Nor did he at any point give way to hatred or bitterness, and when the grotesquely unjust capital sentence of Pilate was being carried out he asked God to forgive his murderers.

So much we know about Jesus on evidence which few historians would wish to challenge. But about what happened afterwards people tend to hold views which are determined more by the beliefs about Jesus which they hold already as Christians or non-Christians, than by the historical evidence which the New Testament provides. Christians have perhaps believed too readily that God gave back life to the corpse of Jesus and removed it from the tomb. Non-Christians have asserted too dogmatically that any rising from the dead is impossible. The evidence of the New Testament needs to be looked at quietly and carefully.

Some New Testament writers, notably the authors of the Gospels, plainly state that the physical body of Jesus was raised from the tomb, and that Jesus was restored to life in so completely physical a way that he was able to take a meal with his friends. But other things that these same writers say, for instance that the risen Jesus could appear and disappear at will, are not quite consistent with this positive assertion of a physical resurrection. And the apostle Paul, whose informants were at least as close in time to the actual events as those of the Gospel-writers, and perhaps closer, makes no reference at all to the removal of Jesus' body from the tomb, and may never even have heard of it. He supposed that Jesus after his death, when he spoke with his friends, had a new body, which he calls a 'spiritual body', especially given to him by God for the purpose—not composed of flesh and blood, and not the same as the body which they had previously known.

It is clear that those who had met the risen Jesus were hard put to it to describe how he had risen from the dead. This was not, for them, the most important thing. For what they wanted to convey was that he *had* risen from the dead—that Jesus himself, in person, had talked to them, given them instructions, promised never to leave them and filled them with a new power. In fact, it was on the (to them) undoubted fact that Jesus was alive and active that they based the whole message that they went round the world announcing to all and sundry.

People today require very strong evidence for such an astonishing event as the resurrection of Jesus Christ before they are ready to believe that it really happened. The evidence is as strong as it can be, and it comes from those who had first-hand knowledge of what occurred. And we can add to it this fact: if Jesus did not rise from the dead we are dealing with a dream or a hallucination. Is it really likely that the whole life of the disciples was permanently changed by something of that sort? Is it likely that so many people, including many of the very wisest, have been deceived in this way ever since?

For most Christians the resurrection of Jesus is absolutely basic to their faith; for others it remains a little doubtful, and needs to be confirmed as they go deeply into what their faith involves. But we cannot escape the fact that for New Testament Christians it is not something to be accepted or rejected, but an essential part of the Gospel for which they were ready to die.

But what sense does all this about Jesus Christ make for us who have to live in a quite different age? After all, a great deal has happened in the world since his time; the structure of society is quite different, our standards of living have been completely changed; we live in a time when science and technology have taken over the provision for many needs for which the people of the ancient world had no resources except to pray to their God or gods.

In spite of these obvious facts which they cannot deny, Christians believe that the life and teaching of Jesus make sense of human life today in a way in which nothing else does. They do not say that we always have to put our convictions in the words that Jesus used, though many of these are not out of date in the least; nor do they say that we have to do, literally and exactly, what he did and asked his friends to do. But they do say that his interpretation of the world, of God and of the human race, makes sense; and that the way of living which he commended has never been improved upon and is never likely to be.

He taught that God is the creator of the universe and the sovereign and father of all men—and when we say that he taught something, we do not refer only to his words; we have in mind the whole direction of his life, and his whole attitude to people as expressed in all his relationships. He taught by what he was and did, as well as by what he said.

To call God the creator was not a new idea. The Old Testament is full of it; so much so that Jesus did not have to repeat it in so many words. He took it for granted, and built on it. It means that everything that exists in the whole universe depends wholly on God for its existence; God wills it to exist, and therefore it does exist. If he stopped willing it to exist (which, so far as we know, he is not likely to do!), it would cease to exist forthwith. This is true whether the universe came into existence after an enormous explosion of energy, or has always existed in a steady state—which of these is the correct account is a scientific question, not a religious one. In either case, creation is not something which happened once and for all a long, long time ago; it is going on all the time—God is for ever creating new things, new living creatures, new people.

Thus we all depend on him, and if it were not for him we should not be here at all. It can be put this way:

The universe minus God = nothing.
God minus the universe = God.

This argues his endless power, knowledge and wisdom. It argues also that he is the ultimate source of truth and goodness and beauty. It asserts therefore the absolute sovereignty of God over the universe and over everything and everyone in it.

But Jesus taught that the creator and sovereign God is also father. 'Father' to a Jew of Jesus' time implied a union of authority and love, for a Jewish father expected his children to obey him. But a good father exercises his authority with infinite respect and compassion for those who are subject to him; he gives them freedom of choice; he helps them to grow up to be complete and free people, and if they go wrong he uses every means, short of taking away their freedom, to bring them back to truth and goodness; and when they come back, he welcomes them with open arms. This, said Jesus is exactly true of God, who is better than the best conceivable human father.

And where does this leave man, so absurdly small in comparison with the vast universe and the infinite power of God? Jesus taught that in spite of his minimal size, his short life, his limited knowledge and his many weaknesses, every member of the human race is of infinite and equal value to God. God creates him to grow to maturity in close relationship to himself and his fellow men, cares for him at every point of his existence and never withdraws his love for him.

Man has freedom, either to respond to the love of God by living in friendship with him, or to repudiate God's intentions for him and find his own independent way through life. Jesus recognised the strong, perhaps innate, tendency in each of us to want his own way, and so to cut himself off from God—even to rebel violently against God. But he insisted that it was always open to us to change our minds and return to friendship with God, and he persistently invited his hearers to do this, saying even that there was more joy in God's heart over one sinner that repented, i.e. changed his mind, than over ninety-nine good people who did not need to repent. And it was to proclaim in the clearest possible terms the unstinted love of God for man that he carried through his chosen policy of unselfish love to the bitter end, which was death by crucifixion.

Thus he pointed to the real meaning of human life. If a loving God is in control of the universe, and his purpose is to bring human beings into a close relationship with himself and each other, and if this love for us is individual and persistent, then we fulfil our nature and make sense of our existence only if we respond to his love and live in his way. The message of Jesus, though at first sight dreamy and worldly, is in fact absolutely realistic and down to earth, and can be worked out as a system which satisfies the sharpest intelligence. In this way Jesus makes sense of God and man.

Jesus Christ is God made Man

THE effect of Jesus Christ on the history of the world is extraordinary on any reckoning. His career as a teacher was, after all, very short—a mere three years at most. It took place in an obscure region of a large empire, and during its whole course it made no sort of a stir outside a very narrow area. He was a Jew, and Jews were then universally regarded as the exponents of a religion and a culture which were of little interest to anyone except themselves. He created a community of friends, but no organisation with committees and funds. No literature on the subject of his work or message appeared until at least fifteen years after his death, and then it was privately circulated among those who belonged to the groups formed by his followers. The manner of his death, though in other countries and circumstances it might have made him into a hero among militant nationalists, since it was carried out by a foreign, oppressive power, in fact discredited him among his own people, since crucifixion was regarded by them as a divine punishment. From the Roman point of view, he was just another tiresome rebel eliminated.

Yet he first, by a steady process, captured the best minds of the later Roman Empire, and persuaded its administrators that he alone could hold the civilised world together. Next, his representatives became largely responsible for the direction which European history was to take and the spirit which was to inform it for a thousand years. His influence was often diluted by alien elements, and his representatives sometimes perverted his message. Partly as a result of this, his Church in Europe became bitterly divided at the end of the Middle Ages. Even after this the history of each European nation was still vitally affected by what was claimed to be his teaching, although by this time various versions of this were abroad. Meanwhile his influence gradually spread to the countries of the new world across the Atlantic, and later to the ancient cultures of Asia and Africa.

In the Third World, and particularly in Africa, the new leaders have been in many cases trained in the Christian tradition. What will emerge from the period of upheaval through which the new nations are passing is highly uncertain; but there is a possibility that in several of them Christ will be found to play a leading role, in spite of the counter attractions of Communism and Western materialism.

Even in Western and Eastern Europe, and in America, his message and his name remain powerful. Even his enemies and the enemies of his Church dare not leave him out of account. On the contrary, poetry and drama, political and ethical discussion, by constant allusion to him, whether friendly or hostile, show that he exercises a pervasive influence over the mind and imagination of modern people; and the persecution of Christians which still goes on indicates that he is a force still very much to be reckoned with.

Meanwhile, all through history since his time and

down to the present moment, individuals and groups of people have acknowledged that he furnished the inspiration of their lives. With his love as their principal motive they have lived lives of consistent integrity and active goodness, and devoted themselves to the welfare of their fellow men.

Of these undoubted facts, which to some people are unpalatable, and to others still almost incredible, the early Church offered the explanation in advance. It said that Jesus is God made man. Without, of course, knowing what lay in store for the human race, but certain that God had his plan for it, Paul and Peter and John and the others asserted that Jesus of Nazareth, whom many of them had known personally, was God at work on earth as a man, who had died and risen again for the salvation of all men. And they were so sure of this that they also believed that Jesus, having left the earth for a time, would shortly reappear and conclude the whole process of human history in God's name.

They were shown by events to be wrong about the shortness of the time before Jesus came back, but on their statement that Jesus is God, and that he will in due course judge the whole human race and all its successes and failures, the Church since their time had stood firm and still stands firm.

These are strange things to believe. Phrases like 'God made man' and 'the salvation of all men' are so far outside our everyday experience that we need to ask very searchingly what they mean. Every generation of Christians has tried to find ways of putting their meaning into familiar and easily understood terms, but what makes sense to one age often makes nonsense to the next. The most famous and longlasting way of indicating their meaning is found in the

Nicene Creed, which most Churches say at the service of Holy Communion: 'We believe in one Lord, Jesus Christ, the only Son of God, eternally begotten of the Father, God from God, Light from Light, True God from True God, begotten not made, of one Being with the Father.' This was published in A.D. 381, and few people today could immediately explain what it is all about. Yet it is not mumbo-jumbo. The people who composed it remembered that Jesus had spoken of God as his father, and claimed that he knew God personally in a way that no one else did. So they concluded that Jesus had not come into existence after his father, but was just as eternal as he was; and so they said that 'Jesus is the only Son of God, eternally begotten (that is, eternally the Son) of the Father'. But they could not possibly say that there were two Gods—the Father and the Son; and claimed therefore that the Father and the Son, though distinguished from each other, are the same eternal Being, one God.

That was quite a mouthful for them, and is still more a mouthful for us. But we can see that they were using the best language they had to express what no language can really express; for how can human language do justice to the nature of God?

We have to try to express the same truth in words that we understand. There is only one God—that goes without saying. But the one God is a much more complex being than any human being. Within the being of God there is the Father, who is also the Creator of all; and there is the Son, Jesus Christ, also a real person, who came to live and die and rise from the dead on this earth at a particular time in history. There is also the Holy Spirit, of whom there will be much more to say later. Jesus came with God the Father's authority, and God the Father takes full responsibility for what Jesus did; and Jesus disclosed in all that he did the character and the purposes of God.

This can be put in many other ways. The infinite love of God is beyond human powers to understand; the only way in which the human race could understand the love of God was by seeing it embodied in a human life. So the Son, Jesus, came to live a human life. Jesus was really human; he thought, he felt, he was happy and he suffered, as a man; he was tempted as a man; he had the knowledge and the ignorance of a man—and, of course, of a man of the first century A.D. In this way he showed to us perfectly the love of God.

It is a little as if Jesus the Son had decided to paint a portrait of himself. But it was impossible to do this in paints on canvas; it had to be done in terms of a real human life—lived by a man with human feelings, human relations, and all the pressures of human society upon him. So the life of Jesus is his self-portrait. All of his wisdom, power and love that can be compressed into a human character and into human experience is to be seen there.

Jesus did not become a man simply to give us a vision of God. That by itself would certainly have made his dangerous journey well worth while. But he had something else in view, something even more important. Life without a vision of God is a meaningless affair; but life with a vision of God, if we are for ever conscious that however hard we try we can never be equal to it or live up to it, can be also terribly frustrating—even wholly devastating. Jesus chose to live a human life, not only to enlighten us and inform us about the character of God, but also to make us able to respond to God in the kind of lives we live and the kind of people we are. Anyone in the least bit honest with himself knows that his intentions, aspirations and professions are considerably in advance of his actual performance—in fact, sometimes directly opposite to them. We do not need only to be pointed towards God, though we certainly need that; we need also to be liberated from our ingrained prejudices, our towering selfishness and our feebleness in the face of emotional or bodily temptation.

But we are not just individual people; we have not got full control of our lives, however strong we may be, because we are constantly influenced and moulded by the kind of society in which we live, and the kind of people with whom we spend our time—quite apart from the impulses and tendencies which we inherit from our parents and our ancestors. The effect on us of our social environment is quite enormous. If we are born in a Catholic slum in Belfast we become in many important ways quite different people from what we should be if we had been born of the same parents in Dublin.

This means that radical changes need to be made in us if we are to do the will of God; but that even radical changes in us are not enough—there have to be radical changes in society also. And that goes for everyone and all society. No one can do the whole will of God for himself unless he lives in a world which makes it possible—a world in which he can be truly and freely himself, with all his powers fully developed and properly used. Racial discrimination, the denial of freedom of thought and speech, the restriction of educational opportunity (as in those countries where black children are virtually not allowed to go beyond a certain stage, if they have education at all), disqualification on grounds of sex —these and all other forms of oppression in our world cramp and cripple the human possibilities even of tough and adventurous people, and leave ordinary people with no chance at all of growing into full maturity. They are not free to achieve the ideal portrayed in Jesus Christ. And it is not only the victims of an inhuman system, not only the oppressed, who are handicapped in this way; the administrators of the system, the oppressors, are also held down and corrupted by the system which they have to administer. The guards as well as the prisoners in a concentration camp are slaves.

This is something of what the New Testament writer had in mind when he said that 'the Father sent the Son to be the Saviour of the World'. The words 'save', 'saviour' and 'salvation' have lost much of their real meaning in religious circles, and nowadays call up the idea of a private, and often rather sentimental, relationship between someone and God.

Salvation is what the New Testament is nearly all about. But it includes far more than most people usually think. It includes God's forgiveness of those who have cut themselves off from him by their self-centredness or carelessness, and are really sorry about their sins; it includes the growth in Christian character of those who have been forgiven; it includes the building up of a community in which everyone can play a full and free part and at the same time concern himself with the interests of others; it includes the liberation of the oppressed, the making and carrying out of just laws, the sharing

39

of the world's resources among all members of the human race according to their needs and the establishment of global peace.

The whole work of salvation was put by God into the hands of Jesus. He undertook it out of love for mankind and by the power of the Holy Spirit. He undertook it, but he did not complete it—as one look at the newspapers, or into our own lives and the lives of our friends, will show. What he did was to release into the world and make effective in human lives the love by which alone people are changed and the world is changed—the love of God for man, and the answering love of man for God and his fellow men.

The cross on which he died is the proof and symbol of this. As we have seen already he did not become man simply in order to die on the cross—though some Christians have thought this. He became man in order to live the life of love in the conditions of his time; and his crucifixion was the result. If man had responded to his love it would not have been. His life, his message, his sufferings and his death were all of a piece and make one whole; and the fact that he was raised from the dead shows that he had actually done what he set out to do: he had conquered death and evil, and he had brought salvation to the world, to individual people and to the whole of human society.

There has been much argument and no conclusion as to how his life and death brought salvation to the world. There are several suggestions in the New Testament which throw light on this, but no final statement. One way of beginning to answer the question is to say that he allowed, once and for all, the pent up evil forces in the human personality and in human society—all the selfishness, cruelty, ambition, pride, hatred, irresponsibility—to come together and vent themselves on him, and thus submitted his love for God and man to the grimmest possible test. If Jesus had turned on his enemies and cursed them, then his love would have been shown to be limited and in the end impotent. But he did not, in fact, do so. He died with a prayer for their forgiveness on his lips. So his love was shown to be triumphant and all-powerful in the darkest moment of his life. Love, we now know, is stronger than hatred and death, the greatest evils of all; it cannot therefore be defeated.

This same love has transformed millions of individual lives and many areas of human society. As Dietrich Bonhoeffer said to his friends as he was taken to the scaffold: 'For me this is the end but also the beginning; I believe in the principles of our universal Christian brotherhood which rises above all national interests, and that our victory is certain.'

The work of salvation, launched by Jesus, is continued by him with his Church in the strength of the Holy Spirit. Meanwhile it is open to everyone to make this salvation his own here and now by a personal act of faith and commitment. Everyone can accept forgiveness; in everyone who receives him Christ carries out his saving work. In this sense, we can all be saved here and now. But we are all aware that our personal salvation is by no means complete; and in a deeper sense we are not and cannot be saved until the whole world is saved, for we all share in the frustrations and failure of humanity—and the full salvation for which Jesus died is in the future. This is summed up in the words of the

Great Thanksgiving in the modern Methodist Communion Service:

> Christ has died,
> Christ is risen,
> Christ will come again.

'We believe that he will come to be our Judge' says the ancient hymn that we call the Te Deum. This also is part of Christian belief. There is an old lady known to the author who wakes up every morning with the thought 'perhaps he will come today', and hopes he will. But this does not sound very sensible; and when certain people go on to say that he will appear in the sky over Salt Lake City, Utah, USA (as the Mormons think)—or some other particular place —it sounds less sensible still. But the old lady and the Mormons have read their Bible, and it does say things like that, but without the reference to Salt Lake City.

The mistake is to take what the Bible says, and what Jesus says, about the future as an exact, literal account of what is going to happen—a kind of newspaper report in advance. Nobody knows the details of the future, and when Jesus and the apostles wished to express their convictions about it, they naturally used the 'picture' method of describing it —as in a parable, which expresses the basic truth, but does not go into particulars.

The basic truth which the New Testament expresses about the future is first that God, and not man, will determine when human events on this earth are to come to an end. We are sometimes afraid that a nuclear explosion caused by man— or the exhaustion of the earth's resources by man—

will bring everything here to an end; we are sometimes cheerfully confident that we can make the necessary arrangements to keep human history going for ever. The New Testament denies both these propositions, and asserts that the matter is at God's disposal, not ours. How he will bring things to an end is not known; that he will do so is not in dispute for Christians.

Second, when that event does take place, the judge of human character and achievements will be (as, indeed, it is already) Jesus Christ the Son of God. What sort of people we really are, what kind of success or failure human beings have made of the responsible task of ordering their own affairs, will be decided by him. The judgement of the leader-writers in *The Times*, the judgement of our friends, the judgement of historians, the judgement of posterity, though they have to be taken fairly seriously at present, will at that point be irrelevant.

This prospect has sometimes terrified Christians and others out of their wits. Understandably so, for we are all afraid of what will happen when our secret thoughts are brought out into the open and seen with the clear eyes of impartial justice. But the judge will be Jesus—not some remote, implacable, abstract, legalistic autocrat, but Jesus, merciful, compassionate, as well as utterly just. Jesus, the Saviour and friend, does not change his character as he fulfils the role of the Judge of all men.

Belief in the Second Coming of Jesus, so long as it is understood as a parable, not a detailed account, of the future, is ground for optimism, not gloom. Our world, for all its upheavals and outrages, is in all-powerful, safe and loving hands after all.

Contrary to all reasonable probability, Jesus, the

martyred prophet from Nazareth, became and remains a person of world-wide influence and significance. For Christians he is also the eternal Son of the Father, God from God, Light from Light, God made man, the divine Saviour of the World, and the compassionate Judge of all. And this belief is based not on wild speculation, but on a careful interpretation of the facts.

3

God is Still at Work

SOMEONE who has read the last few pages might very well say something like this: 'It's all very well to talk about the goodness and the love of God. I can see plenty of evidence for this when I look at the life and character of Jesus. But when I see people starving, or killed by an earthquake, or dying of cancer in a house near by, it's not quite so obvious that God is good. Take that hymn with a pleasant tune which we have to sing at Harvest Festivals, and which contains a verse which runs: "Yes, God is good, all nature says". *All* nature says nothing of the sort! *Some* of nature says it, but certainly not all.'

A very important point is being made here. There are far too many atrociously evil things happening in the world—wars and murders and many other kinds of violence, open and secret, as well as natural disasters—for us to sit back comfortably and say 'God's in his heaven; all's right with the world', as the song goes in Browning's 'Pippa Passes'.

In fact, in the face of this, how can we still say that God is love? We are here right up against one of the hardest problems ever set. If God is good, why is there so much evil in the world? After all, a good God would surely have stopped all evil things from happening. But wait a moment. Would he? If anyone is thoroughly bad, he hates all good things, and stops them if he can. If anyone is thoroughly good, he hates all evil things, but he does not always stop them if he can. He knows that he often cannot stop them without interfering with people's freedom of choice between good and evil; and this freedom of choice is a good thing which he does not wish to interfere with. So he does not wish bad things to happen, of course; but he allows people to use their freedom of choice, and to do bad things if they really want to. Anyone with good parents will confirm this!

So we can understand why many bad things happen although God is perfectly good. They happen, not because God wants them to happen, but because in his goodness he has given human beings the right to choose whether to do right or to do wrong. But this does not completely answer our question. Granted that much, probably most, of the evil in the world is caused by human wrongdoing, there is still a great deal that seems not to be connected with it. No human being is responsible, so far as we know, for tornadoes or earthquakes, or for the anopheles mosquito whose bite causes malaria.

We can at least say this by way of explanation. For anyone to have real freedom of choice, he must know that what he does will have certain results; and for him to know that his action will have certain results, the world in which he operates must be reliable, that is, in that world the same result must always come from the same action and the same cause must always have the same effect. Certain laws must operate. God, in his goodness, because he wishes us to have real freedom of choice, has provided this reliable universe and arranged for it to work ac-

46

cording to certain laws. Now, in a reliable universe, when a mosquito—presumably in quest of nourishment—bites a human body, malaria is likely to follow. We have now learned the way to neutralise the effect of the bite fairly effectively. A rift in the earth's crust is likely in due course to produce an earthquake, and to kill some of the people who live in that part of the world (but they should perhaps have been living elsewhere). A cancerous growth in a human body had dangerous effects until we learn how to check it. And so on. This regular sequence of cause and effect is necessary for human freedom, and good people cannot wish to be exempt from it.

Of course, a big question still remains, which could remain unanswered until the end of time. Why do these mosquitoes and earth-rifts and cancers exist at all? It is hard to see how they perform a useful purpose. But it may be that as we come to know more of the total design of the created universe, even this puzzle will be solved. In the Book of Job this problem is the main theme, and the conclusion is that the matter is beyond human understanding, since the mind of God is ultimately a mystery.

Meanwhile, belief in a good God urges us on to fight evil in all its forms and to strengthen good wherever we find it. We are fortified in this by the knowledge that this is exactly what Jesus did—all through his life and to the point of death. Besides, our belief in God tells us that God's purpose embraces not only this world in which we live at this moment, but the world to come; so that the evil which here seems to triumph can and will be defeated in the end. Since God is love, evil will be eliminated and goodness will be finally supreme.

We cannot claim to have solved all the problems

47

which revolve around the presence of evil in the world, and meanwhile we live our life on the battle-field between good and evil. The battle is sometimes so fierce that we need a good deal of encouragement. We have strong evidence that God in Jesus has grappled with evil in the past; we need to be sure that God is still continuing the struggle. Christians have sometimes slipped into the way of feeling that God was obviously active some time ago, and brought about some spectacular results, but has now retired from the fray, leaving us to carry on by ourselves. This way of feeling has turned many Christians into backward-looking nostalgics, always hankering after the good old days. Remembering the past, and remembering what God has done, is a very good thing, for it is by looking back at the past, the history of Israel and particularly the life and death of Jesus, that we find the clue to what God is doing now and will do in the future. But remembering the past for its own sake, and never getting beyond it, does not help us to understand what is happening here and now, or to live in the present. In Sydney Carter's words:

'Your holy hearsay is not evidence;
Give me the Good News in the present tense.'

Of course that is what we want. What is God doing *now*? The answer to that is a description of the work of the Holy Spirit. We saw in the last chapter that within the being of God, always existing, is God the Father, the creator; the Son, Jesus Christ, whom we recognise in his humanity; and the Holy Spirit. The Holy Spirit is the name we give to God always active in the world. The Holy Spirit is 'he',

48

not 'it'—not a force or a power, but a personal being. Within the complex unity of the one God he continues the work which he begun in creation and brought to a climax by Jesus. And always he acts as a person dealing with persons.

So God's creating work is still going on. Every baby born, every new invention, every idea that comes to life in someone's mind, every healthy development in the structure of human society, every poem or play or picture that catches something new about the meaning of life, every sculpture or building whose shape reveals or realises another human possibility, is the work of the creative Spirit of God. He usually works with us, not separately from us. God creates us with the unique power to be creators —or at least, sub-creators. So when he creates, we are invited to create with him. No doubt, be could do better without us, if he wished to have it that way. Few works of art and few achievements, even of genius, are without flaws, for human ignorance and selfishness keep on intruding themselves. But the Holy Spirit clearly thinks that the risk is well worth taking and prefers to work with us in spite of it.

God's work within the human personality, and in human relations, also continues. Every life redirected into useful channels, every conquest of a temptation or a demoralising habit, every success in becoming a real, authentic person, no longer subject to the dominance of fashion, or prejudice, or someone else's possessive personality, every advance in personal relationships, is an example of this. Every liberation of human beings from oppression, economic, political, radical, sexual, is an act of the Holy Spirit.

Some Christians are eager to 'save souls', that is, to help people to accept the forgiveness of God and live lives according to the example of Christ, and give all their time and energy to that; while others are equally eager to get rid of apartheid, and all other forms of discrimination and injustice and give all their time and energy to that. This is because each group sees the Holy Spirit especially at work in that one sphere of life which it thinks particularly important. It would be better if both groups saw the Holy Spirit equally at work in both spheres, for this is the truth of the matter. This would lead to much greater mutual respect between people with different work to do under the guidance of the same Spirit. The Holy Spirit is involved in all God's work for man and with man.

The Spirit is equally ready to work with groups and with individuals. The group may be large or small, the individual may be clever or dull; the Holy Spirit is available in any case, and himself prompts the good work that has to be done. There is a prayer in the New Testament that the Church may have 'fellowship in the Holy Spirit' (2 Corinthians 13.14); the word for 'fellowship'—a favourite word among Methodist Christians, but, of course, widely used by others—means 'sharing', and the idea is that the Holy Spirit offers a vast reservoir of resources in which we share with all our fellow Christians. The prayer has been granted down the centuries, both to the Church as a whole, in spite of its many failures, and to small groups within the Church; it has been granted to separate denominations, though the Spirit has made it plain that he wishes the Church to be one and undivided.

It has been the tendency in some Churches to

emphasise unduly the work of the Holy Spirit in individual lives, at the expense of his work in the community of the Church. If we have repudiated this tendency, as we should do, we have to recognise nevertheless that he does work in individuals, renewing and directing their energies, promoting their personal development, and fostering in them the virtues of patience, courage, endurance, gentleness, compassion and especially love.

These virtues, among others, form together what Paul calls the 'harvest of the Spirit' (Galatians 5.22). He also speaks of the 'gifts of the Spirit'. He implies that every Christian has, or is given, at least one of these gifts. The list of gifts that he provides is very varied. In fact, he gives two lists, in Romans (12.6–8) and 1 Corinthians (12.4–11 and 12.27–13.1), and they only partly overlap. The first list includes 'inspired utterance', which is what 'prophecy' means in the New Testament, administration, teaching, oratory, the distribution of money to the needy and leadership. The second list includes wise speaking, the expression of the deeper kinds of knowledge, faith to a special degree, healing, miracle-working, inspired utterance (as before), the power to distinguish between various claimants to truth, speaking with tongues, the interpretation of those who speak with tongues—above all, faith, hope and love. Even apart from the last three, there is surely something here for everyone, and there is no reason to think that Paul supposes himself to have exhausted the possibilities.

The very modern, quickly growing 'Charismatic Movement', to be found in all Churches, has done a great service to them all by recovering and expressing an emphasis on the gifts of the Spirit which had been largely lost. It may have done us a disservice, however, by apparently stressing the more spectacular gifts, such as 'speaking with tongues', at the expense of the more humdrum ones. Paul makes it very clear that each gift is equally important in its contribution to the welfare of the whole. Teachers and administrators (yes, even administrators) are 'limbs and organs' of the Body of Christ—as well as great preachers and charismatic personalities.

Christian writers sometimes give the impression that the Holy Spirit is active only in the Church. But, as we have seen, he is not so limited. He is active everywhere, wherever he receives any kind of response or co-operation. Where people are set on their own advancement or wealth, where nations are concerned with themselves and the acquisition of territory and power over other nations, where classes and parties and racial groups (majorities or minorities) are devoted to the defeat or repression of other classes and parties and racial groups, it is hard to see how the Holy Spirit can find much to do. Yet even in such cases he may be able to find a way in, since few individuals or groups are wholly selfish. But where there is response, he is ready to guide and co-operate. The action of the Holy Spirit cannot be restricted to Christian contexts, surely, though it is natural to think that his influence is greater when it is openly invited and genuinely acknowledged.

The three greatest gifts of the Spirit are faith, hope and love; these three are offered to all, and the greatest of the three greatest is love. But hope is also a splendid and invaluable gift. It was never more needed than today, when the wastage of the earth's resources, carried out on a vast and continued scale, has thrown a shadow of gloom over the minds of all intelligent and compassionate people, many of whom see no future for the human race beyond the next few years.

It is no good reacting against the doomsters by saying that things cannot be as bad as they say. The evidence they produce is too weighty. But at this point the Christian is bound to announce that he can see no hope for the future except in God. In God he can see clear hope for the future. The human race, or large parts of it, has been brought several times, to our knowledge, to the very brink of self-destruction by the folly and selfishness of men—as at the collapse of ordered government when the Roman Empire broke up, by the Thirty Years' War, by the First and Second World Wars and by the threat to use the hydrogen bomb—but it has never quite toppled over. We are, somehow, still alive today. Some people ascribe this to the direct act of God, some to the efforts of enlightened men. Christians ascribe it to both: to God working in and with men. Therefore always there is hope, hope based on God's actions in the past—and chiefly his liberating act in Christ, but also on his continued action in human affairs by the power of the Holy Spirit.

The Christian hope is twofold, hope for this world and hope for the world to come. In the dark days of the past—and there have been many dark periods of human history—Christians have often despaired of this world and fixed their hope on the next:

> Brief life is here our portion,
>   Brief sorrow, short-lived care
> The life that knows no ending,
>   The tearless life, is there,

is part of a poem written by a monk in the twelfth century who could see nothing but squalor, disease and misery around him, and found no cure for them except in heaven. It might have been written today, although nowadays we have the resources to reduce, and even to eliminate, much of that particular squalor, disease and misery. The trouble is that we doubt if we have the wisdom or the unselfishness to use these resources effectively. But Christians have the hope, based on the past deeds of Jesus Christ and the continuing activity of the Holy Spirit, that a just society in which all men are free, living at peace with each other and equipped to be themselves, will emerge, with the help of the Holy Spirit, in spite of the political and economic turmoil of our times—indeed, with Paul, that the whole created order will 'enter upon the liberty and splendour of the children of God' (Romans 8.21).

But no re-ordering of human society, however just and lasting, can free us from the limits imposed by the fact that our knowledge is incomplete and our earthly life-span short. So there is a second hope implicit in the Christian faith—the hope of a life for human communities and human beings which is really complete and wholly satisfying, of a life in direct relationship with God which knows no limits of time, space or understanding, of a life which begins on earth and is fulfilled in heaven. And this hope is securely grounded in the resurrection of Jesus Christ.

The life—'eternal life'—on which Christian hope is set, does not depend on belief in the 'immortality of the soul'. It is no part of Christian faith that our souls are immortal. In fact, it is rather confusing to talk about our souls at all, for no one quite knows

what a soul is! Christians believe in the 'resurrection of the body'—a Biblical phrase which needs
explaining. The 'body', according to the New Testament, is the *total self*. Our physical frame dissolves
after death; but God gives life to our total selves, and
we, as persons, enter upon it fully in the community
of heaven. Some people may reject this life, to their
infinite loss, but it is the gift of God through Jesus
Christ, always on offer to everyone.

4

The Witnesses: Church, Sacraments and Bible

At the beginning of 'Godspell' a number of people wander about the stage carrying banners bearing such names as 'Socrates', 'Marx', 'Chairman Mao', 'Buddha', 'Christ', 'Nietzsche', 'Aristotle', etc., presumably to indicate the theories that are abroad in the world today. Then the troupe of circus players—for that is what they are—settle down to act out the story of Jesus Christ as it is given in the Gospels. They want to know whether it makes a real impact upon them, really makes sense in their own experience, or is just a tale of long ago.

This was for them the test of the 'Jesus Christ theory'. Does it work out in actual life and experience? Every theory must be put to that test, and so must all the things that have been said in this book. Until that happens, they remain just theory.

This testing has in fact taken place, in two particular ways. First of all, it was put to the test by Jesus himself in the way he lived and the things he did. He was the living expression of what he taught. He did not say, as so many preachers seem to have to, 'pay attention to what I say, not what I do, because I know I do not always practise what I preach'. He could afford to have his teaching tested by what he himself was and did.

All this we know already. But a modern critic could say: 'That was all very well in the time of Jesus, when life was simple. How do we know that the theory worked in later times or will work in our sophisticated and complicated age?' So a second test has to be applied, the test of history, and this is a test which is always going on. To put it briefly, the Church of Jesus Christ, starting in his own time and coming down to ours and continuing into the future, is the testing ground of the Christian view of life. It claims to be all sorts of wonderful things—the Body of Christ and the People of God, for instance—and these claims all add up to an overall claim to be the expression and continuation of Christ's teaching and life. The Church asserts that she is the way by which people in any age, including the present one, can have access to the truth and power of God as he is shown in Christ, and that the Holy Spirit enables the Church to be just that.

In one sense, Jesus founded the Church, and in another sense he did not. He collected a band of friends around him, he taught them his Good News (which is what 'Gospel' means), he showed them how to live out the Good News, he sent them to speak and act in his name, he instructed them to spread the Good News over the widest possible area when he had left them. He told them to welcome and baptise those who came to believe in him, asked for God's forgiveness and adopted the Christian way of life.

In this way Jesus in his own life began the Church. But he did not draw up its precise constitution or method of government, its discipline or its exact orders of worship. He did, however, promise to his friends the continuance of his presence and power among them after his death, and the guidance of the Holy Spirit.

As a result of the preaching of the first disciples, the followers of Jesus grew rapidly in numbers in Jerusalem and beyond, and spread out into the rest of the Roman Empire. So the Church had to think about constitutions, funds, governing bodies, leaders and liturgies. At first there was much variety in all these respects, but by about A.D. 200 the Church had settled down to a system in which three orders of ministry, bishops, priests and deacons, formed the pattern of its administration.

The leadership and the worship of the Church came to be under the control of the first order, the order of bishops, and it was they who gave direction to its devotional life. In course of time, certain 'super-bishops'—'archbishops'—gained pre-eminence over the other bishops in the great centres of Christianity—Constantinople, Alexandria and especially Rome—and in the Western part of the Church the Bishop of Rome, whom we call the Pope, ultimately reached a position of undisputed monarchy. Undisputed for a long time, that is, but the Churches of Eastern Europe were never happy about his pre-eminence, and came to repudiate it. Then in the sixteenth century nearly half of Western Europe broke away from Rome, and one of the issues at stake was the sovereignty of the Pope. The Churches of the Reformation, in England and elsewhere, adopted various systems of government, each claiming to follow the New Testament, some of them retaining bishops, priests and deacons, others insisting that in the one ministry all are of equal status. The Church of England, since the separation from Rome, has preserved the threefold ministry, and sought to combine the traditions of the early Church with the best insights of the Reformers.

The divisions just mentioned have been the source of violent upheavals in the Church from time to time. There have been fierce arguments also about parts of Christian teaching, often very important parts. There have been times of savage persecution, chiefly in early times, but also since then and in our own day, and many occasions when Christians have persecuted other Christians. There have been periods when the Church was prosperous and at least outwardly successful, there have been periods of decline in size, influence and Christian example. Often the Church has been at its best when it has been most persecuted and harassed.

So far it could be said that the testing out of Christian teaching in the life of the Church has not yet clearly demonstrated that it is workable and valid. In fact, there are many episodes—not least the persecutions of Jews—and periods of history from which the opposite conclusion might well be drawn. But there are other elements in the story, equally important. In the time of the early persecutions, when Christianity was fighting and suffering for its life against the organised oppression of Roman emperors, governors and imperialistic interests, the courage of the preachers, the endurance of the martyrs, the fidelity of bishops and clergy to the faith of the New Testament and the devotion of thousands of ordinary people, kept the Gospel alive for future generations and ultimately built it into the foundations of European civilisation. In the so-called Dark Ages, after the Roman Empire's 'decline and fall', Christian monks, thinkers and administrators preserved the substructure of law and morals which prevented complete disintegration, and later erected a system of thought and conduct which formed the fabric of medieval life. In modern times, Christian influences have mingled with other forces, many of them largely Christian themselves in origin, to liberalise and humanise much of Western society, by promoting tolerance, the freedom of the individual, the emancipation of slaves, the growth of schools and hospitals and the breaking down of racial and sexual discrimination. And nowadays the divisions within Christendom itself are on the way to being healed.

Even so, there could still be some remaining doubt about the result of this age-long test of the truth of Christianity. What is decisive in indicating that Christianity has really passed the test which is provided by the Church's life is that the essence of the matter—the teachings that cluster round Jesus himself, and the life which he himself embodied—has been preserved, in spite of everything, by the Church and has come down intact into our own time; it is acknowledged and put into practice by millions of people all over the world today; and it is being constantly revitalised by reference to the sources from which it comes, to be found in the Church and the Bible. So we can say with confidence that Christianity works today.

But we need to study more carefully the way in which the Church conducts its affairs. It has sometimes been almost ruthlessly efficient, sometimes shamblingly incompetent, usually something between the two. At present most denominations, aware at last of the decline in their influence over large masses of people, have become deeply self-critical, and genuinely eager to update their methods and apply their message to the needs of the time. The effort to do this has brought to light a truth of basic Christian faith which had been long forgotten. It is that the Church is really and truly a people, made up of individual persons, but of individual persons bound together into a corporate whole by their love of Christ and their loyalty to to him. It is not primarily an institution, though it has to have an organisation and a constitution and a balance sheet and paid officials; still less is it an association of clergy and ministers with laypeople as their supporters and adherents, though clergy and ministers are an essential part of it. It is a community of people, the people of God. This means that the 'ministry of all Christian people', laypeople and ministers together, is even more important than the ministry of those who have a special ministry by being ordained 'to the ministry of Word and Sacraments'. By the witness and example of the whole body of Christians, the Church stands or falls.

So what is the place of the ordained ministry within the ministry of all Christian people? It is necessary, as is obvious, for the maintenance of the institution, for the continuance of the teaching and for the organisation and carrying out of pastoral care. And for these purposes it needs to be carefully trained and prepared. This is why from the very beginning certain people have been called (by God, as they would claim), and set apart (by the Church) to be apostles, ministers, clergy, priests, deacons, presbyters, superintendents, bishops, whichever form of ministry has been adopted and whichever names have been used. And rightly so: for the original teaching of the Gospel has to be handed down, safeguarded and interpreted, and applied to the needs of each succeeding generation. This can be done only by those who follow each other in an orderly succession of leadership, as happens also in a well-conducted business or school or hospital, and who are closely related to each other by a common allegiance and a mutual loyalty.

But there is another and stronger reason for an ordained ministry. Every body of people needs an ambassador and a focus. Great numbers of people cannot speak their common mind at any given moment; indeed, at any given moment, they probably have not got a common mind. They need someone, or a fairly small group, to formulate and express what they truly believe, but cannot immediately put into thought or words. They need a genuine and trusted spokesman, an ambassador; if they do not have one, they will be at the mercy of an ambitious rabble-rouser who will pretend to speak for them, but really speaks for himself and his own interests. They need also a personal focus of their needs and hopes and convictions and resources—someone who will bring them into unity, remind them of their past and lead them into new enterprises and discoveries.

The New Testament explains that in response to these needs of the Church locally and world-wide, God the Holy Spirit has given to the Church an ordained ministry consisting of those whom he calls; and that he provided those whom he calls with the gifts of mind and spirit which they need for the carrying out of their tasks—and all of this, says Paul (Ephesians 4.12), is 'to equip God's people for work in his service, to the building up of the body of Christ'.

For many centuries Christians have supposed,

rather curiously, that God has limited his choice of those to be ordained to the male sex, as if the sole fact of femininity (in spite of the absence of any Biblical veto) disqualified half the human race, whatever other qualifications the members of that half might have. It may well be that in the early days of the Church the social position of women imposed such a restriction on those available for the ministry. But the disqualification can scarcely have been meant to be permanent, and in recent years many Churches, including the Methodist Church, have begun to ordain women.

The Christian faith, then, was embodied in Jesus Christ, and is preserved and continued down to the present day in the life and witness of all its members, ministerial and lay. But life for each of us is too complex, too full of what are truly called 'temptations', for us to go steadily from stage to stage and task to task by simply using our native resources. We need strength and nourishment to keep us going. This nourishment for our inner selves is offered to us by God, and conveyed to us through what are called sacraments. A sacrament is a physical object or action through which what is more than merely physical is conveyed to us. We are familiar with this sort of thing in many areas of life. Nations have their flags and national anthems; clubs and colleges have their coats-of-arms and colours; marriage is symbolised by a ring or rings. These are not merely outward indications or reminders of what the organisations stand for. In varying degrees they help to make real in people's lives what they symbolise— patriotism, or club loyalty, or married harmony.

But the Christian sacraments, though they are similar in some ways to these 'signs and symbols', have something much more valuable and important to give. The two sacraments of the Gospel, Baptism and Holy Communion (or the Lord's Supper, or the Eucharist) convey to us the needed strength for our Christian life and are given to us for this purpose by Jesus Christ himself.

They convey it to us in different ways. Baptism means a gift given to us straight away, and a promise of more to come in the future—entry into the Church now, and the growth of new life in the Church from now on. Infants are baptised, not because they have faith in Christ, which they clearly have not, but because God loves them and welcomes them long before they are in a position to respond to that loving welcome, for God does not wait for our response before he acts; nor does his love for us depend on our faith. Those who delay baptism until the one to be baptised knows and accepts what is happening are perhaps laying too much stress on what we are able to do, and too little on what God does, in baptism.

Baptism happens only once; but the Lord's Supper is taken again and again. Baptism is like birth into a family, in this case the family of the Church. The Lord's Supper supplies the regular nourishment we need for sustaining our Christian life. But though the act of baptism is once-for-all, it is the beginning of a process in which we turn away from selfishness and grow into the new life which Christ gives us.

The Lord's Supper has been celebrated so many times in so many places by Christians with so many different approaches that it is quite difficult to get down to the real core of what happens when the minister takes the bread, gives thanks, breaks the bread and gives it to the people. But this reminder of the four things which he does in the manner of Jesus at the Last Supper leads us some way towards the heart of the matter. Jesus asked his friends to do in the future what he had just done at his farewell supper, and to do it 'in remembrance of him'. To English ears this sounds as if he simply wanted them to have a memorial feast in his honour from time to time—as might be held for any martyred hero—and this is in fact what some Christians have understood Holy Communion to be. But such an interpretation misses the real meaning of the word that Jesus used for 'remembrance'. On the real meaning of that word, to 'remember' Jesus is to do much more than remember him: it is to recall him into the present time, to bring him alive again in our present circumstances. Of course, he is not dead; so he cannot be literally 'brought alive'. But he can and does come to us to be the host at his supper as a living personal reality from whom we can receive once again his gift of himself; he is alive for us at that moment as at no other time. There is no need to spend a long time in arguing as to whether or not the bread and wine become his body and blood. This is for some Christians impossible to believe, to others it makes good sense. The important thing is that he, Jesus, is present, and that we are his guests.

Nor is it only we, who may be a mere handful, who are present as his guests. The Lord's Supper is the 'holy communion' of all Christian people; it is the festival of the whole Church, in heaven and on earth. And that is true whether we meet in a massive cathedral, a village Bethel or a friend's lounge.

Another aspect of the same truth can be put in a different way. Jesus died on the Cross and rose again for the whole human race; this was the sacrifice of himself for the 'sins of the whole world'. That sacrifice cannot be repeated; it has happened once and for all. But it is brought into direct and present relevance to us as we eat and drink 'in remembrance of him', and all that was done for us by Christ is ours for the taking—that is, forgiveness and new life. The whole action of God in Christ for the salvation of mankind becomes ours in the present time.

The argument of this book up to now makes it necessary at this point to ask a very serious question. What is the original evidence for these many statements about God the Father, about Jesus Christ the Son, and about the Holy Spirit? Granted that Christians down the ages have tested all these statements in their own life and experience and found that they are sound. Granted that the Church in its many forms has discussed them and defended them and clarified them over a very long period of history, and is convinced that they give a true account of God's dealings with the human race. Where do they come from in the first place and can we trust the source from which they come?

It is clear that they depend a great deal on the evidence provided by the Bible. It is easy to find people who will say that the Bible is not to be trusted, or even that it is made up of fables that no sensible person can take seriously. Such remarks spring from some confusions of thought. It is perfectly true that it is no longer possible, except by stretching human willingness to believe a very long way, to accept as literal truth every statement that the Bible makes. Without doubt, quite a number of historical mistakes have been discovered, and the Bible from time to time says things which are made highly questionable by our present-day scientific knowledge. But it is not very sensible to argue, as some people do, that, because there are some mistakes in the Bible, the Bible cannot be believed at all. Not even *The Times*, or the greatest historians and scientists that have ever been, are entirely free from error! But we do not therefore at once decide that nothing that they say is to be trusted. We simply go on applying to their statements the usual tests of truth.

There is another confusion of thought about the Bible into which some people fall. They say that they cannot possibly believe that the world was made in six days, or that Jonah was swallowed by a fish and then released alive, or that Jesus went physically up into the sky till he became invisible; so they dismiss the early chapters of Genesis, and the book of Jonah, and the first chapter of Acts, as incredible. They have failed to distinguish two different kinds of truth. There is truth of fact: it is found in statements which describe events which can be seen and heard, and photographed and televised. There are, of course, many such statements in both the Old and the New Testaments, and they have to be checked as carefully as possible, especially as most of them were first made before there was much machinery for verifying historical and scientific statements.

There is also the truth conveyed by a story or parable which does not claim to be literally true. There are many examples of this in the Bible and each is intended to express a basic truth about God, the world and man. Such basic truths can sometimes be set out in philosophical or theological statements, and there are some of these in the Bible, and many more in modern literature. But basic truths are far more likely to be understood by ordinary people if they are told in the form of a story. The early chapters of Genesis, the book of Jonah, the narratives of the ascension of Jesus, and very many other parts of the Bible, including the parables of Jesus, are 'stories' of this sort. To say this is not to say that they are untrue. On the contrary, it is to claim a very important kind of truth for them; it is to claim that they tell us some basic things about the universe.

With these confusions cleared out of the way, it is much easier to see what the Bible really is. It is a collection of books of many different kinds—histories, poems, hymns, letters, Gospels. They all have one purpose: to set out with the greatest possible force a particular view of God, the world and mankind. The subject is God, the world and man; and everything else it contains—history, literature and teaching on conduct and behaviour—is subordinate to this. The Jews acknowledge the Old Testament only, and, taken by itself, it sets out the Jewish faith. Christians add the New Testament to the Old, and call the result one book—the book which sets out the Christian faith. For Jews the Old Testament is complete in itself; for Christians the Old Testament needs to be completed (and at some points corrected) by the New, and to be understood in the light of the New.

There is no radical clash between the two Testaments, though there is sometimes a clash between individual statements in them, certainly if they are taken out of their historical context. The New Testament takes for granted, and often does not trouble to repeat, a great deal of the Old Testament. Yet from the Christian point of view the full meaning of the Old Testament cannot be seen until the story of Jesus ties it together and brings it to a climax.

The Bible as a whole shows that God has been dealing with man all through history ever since he first appeared on the earth. So it is through the history of the human race that God's dealings with man can best be described. This is what the Bible sets out to do, and its description reaches its climax in the coming of Jesus, his career and the events which flowed from it. The scheme of it can be seen if we set it out in the form of a historical drama, in four acts, with a prologue and an epilogue, somewhat like this:

Prologue: the creation of the universe and man, followed by man's choice of evil.

Act I: God's choice of Abraham to be the founder of the nation, Israel, through which God would save the world; the early history of that nation until its escape from Egypt.

Act II: the wanderings of the new nation, Israel, its settlement in Canaan and its rise to power. Then the division of the nation and the consequent disasters. The attempts of the prophets to recall Israel to its true destiny, and their failure. The defeat and exile of the two sections of the nations.

Act III: God brings back one part of the nation from exile, and establishes a smaller nation than before to be his agent. Disobedience continues, but a few are faithful, and the hope of God's full salvation is kept alive.

Act IV: Jesus comes to preach and establish

God's rule; he is opposed and killed. He defeats death and evil, and sends his apostles to the ends of the earth. They reach Rome, the centre of the civilised world and the base for all future operations.

Epilogue: The vision of the final battle between good and evil, and of the ultimate victory of God through Jesus Christ.

If this is used as a clue to the understanding of the whole Bible, a great number of individual books and chapters will fall into place, and many puzzling, even contradictory, passages will become much clearer—so long as it is remembered that a collection of books written and compiled over a period of more than a thousand years or so is not likely to be arranged in a tidy order, and that in such a collection all the authors cannot be expected to have exactly the same point of view. The remarkable thing about the Bible is not that there are some differences and inconsistencies, but that there is so solid a consensus among all the writers.

Thus the Bible gives a reliable but not infallible record, with the authority of those who were in a good position to know, of the character of God and his relations with the human race and all its members. Those who wrote this record were inspired, no doubt in varying degrees, by the Holy Spirit, in such a way that their own powers were by no means suspended or abolished, but rather enhanced and developed by the co-operation of their minds and spirits with him. So the Bible can be truly called the Word (not the words) of God.

5

The Christian Style of Life

IT WAS pointed out in the very early days of Christianity that Christians used the same languages, wore the same clothes, ate the same food and lived in the same countries as everyone else, in spite of deep differences of conviction. This situation has not changed. It is true that monks and nuns, and clergymen from time to time, and a few other special groups of Christians, have a way of dressing which is different from that of other people; but the great majority of Christians cannot be distinguished in the streets or the shops or the factories or the offices or on the sea front, or anywhere, by the clothes they wear or usually by the jobs they do. And if the language they use is not so highly coloured as that of those who cannot express themselves without swearing, that applies to many other responsible people who are not Christians.

So a Christian looks and dresses like anyone else, and he behaves like anyone else for a great part of his time. There is no virtue in being different for the sake of being different. There is no call on a Christian to draw attention to himself as a peculiar—still less a superior—person. So is there anything at all special about the Christian's way of life?

Sometimes Christians have been brought up to believe that there is something wrong about enjoying oneself, and that disapproval of pleasure is what marks out a Christian. This is what is usually meant by a Puritan upbringing, though so far as history goes it was only some Puritans who thought like that. But whether Puritan or not, hatred of pleasure is not Christian. It is hardly likely that God would give us the opportunity and encouragement to enjoy so many things, and then condemn us as sinners if we enjoy them. Methodist teachers in the past have often gone wrong on this point, in order, no doubt, to stress the truth that life is a serious business.

What, then, marks out a Christian from other people? It is widely supposed, by Christians and non-Christians alike, that the distinctive mark of a Christian is that he has more rules to keep than a non-Christian. On this view, he keeps the ordinary rules of honourable conduct—he tells the truth, keeps his promises, pays his debts, looks after his wife (or her husband) and children, and keeps the laws; and then adds a few more which the Church requires of him, such as, 'do not gamble, drink or swear', 'do not play games or do any unnecessary work on Sundays', 'do not lose your temper when you are provoked', and 'do not trifle with other people's feelings'.

Once again, it has to be admitted that Christian teachers, mostly belonging to a generation or two before the present one, have suggested that being a Christian essentially consists in keeping rules and regulations designed to prevent them from straying on to the wrong road. They probably did not mean to teach this, but this is the impression that they have given.

In fact, the Christian life is not governed by rules

at all—at least, not by rules in the proper sense of the word. A rule is an instruction about behaviour which you cannot disobey without being a wrong-doer, or, in Christian language, a sinner. The most famous set of rules ever laid down—the Torah, the Jewish law—was derived from the Old Testament, and from the Ten Commandments in particular. At the time of their publication the keeping of the Commandments was known and accepted as Israel's proper response to the acts of God which had made it into a nation. But Israel forgot the original purpose of the Commandments, and turned them into rules to be obeyed in order to find favour with God, with the corollary that if you did not keep them in their entirety you were bound to arouse God's displeasure. By the time of Jesus more and more laws had been added, and the keeping of rules had become the essence of Judaism.

But Jesus and the New Testament writers looked at the whole business of living from a different point of view. They say that we cannot put ourselves by our own efforts in the right relationship with God—Jesus himself had done this for us, as we saw earlier, because we could not manage it for ourselves. The new relationship which Jesus has made possible has to be accepted and worked out in ordinary living. For this the old laws offered useful guidelines; but these guidelines must never again be turned into rules which must at all costs be kept.

Of course, we all need guidelines. We are not clever enough or strong enough to know and do what we should on every occasion without reference to the wise advice that these guidelines offer. But even the best guidelines may go out of date, and often they do not apply exactly to every situation in which we find ourselves; and so we can never be bound by them absolutely.

For a Christian, as Paul says, lives 'not under law but under grace' (Romans 6.14). That is, we are not under the grim necessity of keeping rules which have been laid down for us on pain of losing our chance of being accepted by God. If we were, we should have little hope of reaching the appointed standard, and we should be full of guilty feelings because we had not done so. God has given us his 'grace'—his free, undeserved love, and forgiven us; and now it is in response to his love, and in gratitude for what he has done for us in Christ, and not in obedience to rules, that we do what God wishes us to do and live as he wishes us to live. And the same grace, the same undeserved love of God, shown to us in Jesus, and now continued in the power of the Holy Spirit, makes us capable of doing this and living in this way—far more so than we could ever have managed otherwise. The guidelines are there, and are very useful, and we should think many times before we disregard them; but in the last resort we do what we do out of gratitude and love, as the friends of Jesus, in the freedom of the children of God. We are his sons and daughters, not his slaves.

This leads us on to see that being a Christian is primarily a matter of inner attitudes and relationships; actions and words are important, but they spring from our attitudes and relationships, not the other way round.

Being human means having attitudes to God and other people, and relationships with them. It also means, as we shall see later, having an attitude to ourselves. Since God is more important than any-one and anything in the universe, and since we are never outside his presence, his knowledge and his care, our relationship with him is of absolutely prime importance. All sorts of relationship with him are possible. We may be indifferent, rebellious, contemptuous, complacent, wary, obsequious, rever-ent, obedient or loving, or we may vary between several of these conditions. Most people go through several stages of relationship with him. The Chris-tian's relationship to God at its best is a combination of reverence, obedience and love. Though God, on his side, offers the possibility of this relationship to us, we do not find it easy, because of the elements of pride and selfishness in all of us, to accept and develop it.

This is where worship and prayer come in. Some people say that if our relationship with God is right, we do not need to engage in special acts of worship and prayer. It may even be that some people whose whole life is prayer do not need them, because their relationship with God is so deep and un-troubled. But since Jesus worshipped and prayed, and since the people who seem to be the best Chris-tians follow his example, this is not very likely. We need times of special relationship if our normal relationship is to be permanent and healthy, as in all forms of friendship. We do not remain very good friends with people with whom we do not bother to spend much time.

Yet worship and prayer are not extra activities which we add to an already full life—and which, therefore, we are prone to neglect when other things press upon us. They are essential parts of the full life of a Christian. We are, we hope, responding to the love of God in all parts of our life; at certain times this response becomes open and explicit. We cannot think directly about God all the time without failing to concentrate on what we are supposed to be doing, but unless we make occasions to think directly about God, he may well go out of our minds and lives altogether. But to think directly about God is difficult for us, even if we think about him as he is revealed in Jesus. This is why there are so many aids to worship in words and music and action.

Worship is always corporate, since even when we engage in an act of worship on our own, we are in fact worshipping with the whole Church; we bring into play the thoughts and words of our fellow-Christians, we remember their concerns, we draw on their experience. Whether we are by ourselves, or in a small group, or in a congregation, we are responding with all Christian people to the love of God in Christ, brought home to us in the reading and preaching of the Bible, the prayers and the sacraments.

There is much to be said for doing this according to set forms of service and by the use of words which Christians have valued for a long time; for the truths of the Christian faith and the wisdom of Christians wiser than ourselves are imbedded in the words and prayers that are used. There is also much to be said for spontaneous worship, when we praise the goodness of God by bringing to him the music and the prayers and the actions which best express our experience of God and of life in our everyday affairs. There is nothing to be said for the conventional recital of familiar words, however beautiful, which have lost their point of contact with the life of people today—whether they are said in a splendid cathedral or a village chapel.

Fortunately, in reaction against the tedium of much traditional routine, there have been renewals in all Churches of both 'liturgical' and 'free' worship, so that all who take part are encouraged to take part actively, and to offer themselves with all their best powers to God in response to his love for us.

Prayer can well be defined as 'talking with God', as it is in the Methodist Junior Catechism. This definition at least saves us from supposing that prayer is addressing God with a list of our requirements. We pray when what should be our normal relationship with God comes out into words, and still more into the positive wish to know God's will for us. We also pray when, after a period of forgetting God, we remind ourselves of his presence, and engage in silent or (on our side) verbal conversation with him.

It will be easily seen, and just as easily forgotten, that the object of prayer is to discover the will of God and to be put into harmony with it. This can be a long process, but Christians are committed to it. God knows our needs, and what he plans for us to do; prayer is our chief way of finding out what is in his mind. It is perfectly legitimate for us to tell God what we believe to be our needs, so long as we are really prepared to have any or all of our proposals rejected or corrected. We shall frequently find that God wishes to give us something quite different from what we had thought, but certainly something much better, though we may not at once recognise it as such. But he cannot give it to us unless we are ready to abandon our preconceived ideas and accept it. You may have noticed that good parents have a way of treating us in the same way as God does.

It is in this light that we should think of the traditional fivefold division of prayer into adoration, thanksgiving, confession, intercession (prayer for others) and petition (prayer for ourselves). They are the five elements in the discovery of God's will. It is in this light, too, that we should look at the question: does God answer prayer, and, if so, how? Plainly, quite often, his answer is a simple, 'No, that is not what you need'. But suppose we ask for something which, so far as we can see, is certainly the will of God—the prevention of a war or something like that; are we sure to receive it? It has to be said that we are not. For many other people are involved in the matter, and, however much the Holy Spirit seeks to influence them, God does not overrule them, or force them to abandon their warlike plans; he respects human freedom. Yet even in discouraging cases like these, we have put ourselves on God's side to be used by him as he wishes in the furtherance of peace; our prayers are not wasted.

Our relationships with other people take up a great part of our lives, and it is right that they should. We are told to 'love our neighbour (that is, anyone with whom we have any kind of contact) as ourselves', and we usually love ourselves very much indeed. This is a tall order, but it fortunately does not mean that we have to have warm feelings towards everyone, especially as some of the neighbours we have to love may be people whom we find it hard to like at all! To 'love our neighbour' means to respect him as a person and to further his best interests. We are not just to refrain from attacking him, robbing him, cheating him, blackmailing him and forging his signature: these are minimum duties laid upon everyone. A Christian is asked to go much

78

further, and to respect his personality and his free-dom to the limit, and actively to help him both in times of trouble and in the fulfilment of all the worthwhile aims that he has. Nobody has time to do this for everyone else, of course; but each of us can find a large number of neighbours to 'love' in this way.

This principle of 'treating other people as persons in their own right', as we may put it, applies in every department of life. Not least inside our families, where mutual respect between young and old is a necessary basis for any kind of real happi-ness and real personal development. It applies also to our relationships with the members of the other sex. Indeed, since they form about half the total of the human race, and some of them are likely to en-gage our deepest feelings and fundamentally affect our lives, to fail in our handling of relationships with them may mean failure in many other parts of life as well.

These people fall into three classes. There are those of the opposite sex who affect us as little as most members of our own sex, and there is no special quality in our relationship with them. There are those with whom we share interests and tastes and ideas, and with whom we are are able to work har-moniously and enjoy our common interests. In such a relationship we need to be very sensitive towards each other, for men and women do not think and feel in exactly the same way. Especially do we need to be freed from the undue self-consciousness by which many people are plagued. The principle of respecting each other as true equals applies not least in this area of life.

Then there are those who to a greater or less

degree atract us physically and emotionally, and sometimes fascinate us, at least temporarily, to the exclusion of everything and everyone else. When we are swept off our feet in this way, it is often hard to make wise decisions, and it is useful to do something towards imagining such situations in advance. At one time, not very long ago, people in this situation were often discouraged from meeting each other, or even forbidden to do so—in their own interests, as they were told. This often led to the intensification of emotion, and to ill-considered action as a result. Nowadays the pendulum has swung to the other extreme, and the opposite advice is often given: do what your feelings tell you to do, and if this results in sexual intercourse, so long as proper precautions have been taken, no harm is done. Such advice was at first thought to be wonderfully liberating, after all the vetoes and repressions of the past. But now we can see that to follow such advice often leads to deep frustration and disillusionment for one or both of the people involved, and is a poor preparation for a lasting relationship with a married partner in later life.

So it looks as if the best way of dealing with this very important relationship has still to be found, and it is wrong simply to condemn out of hand those who have made mistakes in their attempts to find it, unless they have been wholly selfish in their approach.

But there is a way forward. Sex, in the sense of a desire for, or the attainment of, a physical relationship, is only one part of human life, though it can easily become the most powerful part, for good or ill. It should never be thought of as something by itself. All of us, deep down, are looking and hoping for a relationship with someone which will be lasting, happy and comprehensive, 'for better, for worse, in sickness and in health, till death us do part'. Such a relationship when we find it will certainly be sexual, and sexually expressed; that will be the most joyful thing about it. But it will also reach into many other parts of life. It will involve an equal partnership in making plans, spending money, bringing up children; it will mean community of interests and friendly companionship; it will mean mutual support in times of illness and trouble, and shared happiness in times of success. Sex in marriage is sex in a total personal relationship, all the richer because it expresses the coming together of two whole people, not just of two bodies. Is not this something worth waiting for?

Surely the best preparation for this is not to treat sex as something on its own and enjoy it regardless, and so develop a taste for sex and yet more sex, and perhaps to find every experience of it unsatisfying and frustrating; but to control our feelings, however strong, until the time of self-commitment to another person in marriage. We are bound to have ups and downs and to make mistakes before we find our true partners, but these need cause no permanent harm so long as we never exploit other people for our purposes or allow them to exploit us for theirs.

It used to be possible to think of our 'neighbour' as all those living in the same town or village or community, since we had little or no contact with those who lived farther away. Now all that is changed, with ease of travel and speed of communications; and now our 'neighbourhood' can comprise the whole world. Thus a Christian's relationships

81

with other people are now very widely extended, and we find ourselves involved in the welfare of people of whose very existence English people were previously unaware. We cannot do everything for everyone, or take the troubles of the whole world on our shoulders; its population and complexity are too large for that. But we can take an informed, intelligent and compassionate interest in those who suffer from oppression, apartheid, discrimination and poverty; and we can do this without neglecting the victims of disease and starvation, or the homeless and deprived people in our own country. Each of them is now our neighbour, a person for whom Christ died. To take this concern seriously lands some Christians in national and international politics, and all Christians in a sustained support of the agencies which seek to liberate the captive and the oppressed. For the Christian there can be no opting out of the long struggle to help the 'poor of the world' towards the full life and full human dignity which God intends for them.

So far we have been trying to put into modern terms the meaning for us of the words of Jesus: 'Love God with all your heart and mind and soul and strength, and your neighbour as yourself'. But being a Christian is not mainly or essentially a matter or doing things—though there are many things to do—but of being a certain sort of person. So we have to have a certain attitude to ourselves. It would in some ways be very useful if it were possible to put together an identikit, an exact model, of a Christian, so that we could compare it with ourselves each day and see how we were doing. But in fact it would be disastrous, because each of us, thank God, is different from everyone else and there is no exact model approved for us to which we are required to conform. It would be extremely monotonous if there were. What we are given is the example of Jesus, which we are to follow in the way that brings out our true selfhood, and this means an infinite variety of Christian people.

But there are some qualities which are basic to Christian living, and if we continue to be deficient in any of these, we are shown to be lacking in certain Christian essentials. These qualities St Paul collects together under the title of 'the harvest of the Spirit', for it is the Spirit who develops and empowers them in each of us. One of them is compassion, which means the ability to get into other people's shoes and understand what they feel and what they need, and to share with them both their happiness and their troubles. Another is gentleness, which once was called meekness, until that word lost all strength and meaning. Gentleness is not softness or weakness or willingness to be pushed around. It depends on the possession of inward power and it consists in the use of that power never to dominate or exploit or patronise, but to build up and to bring out the best in other people. Another is courage, which is not the absence, but the conquest, of fear. Another is patience, which is the willingness to put up with unpleasant things, if necessary for a long time, for the sake of others. And, of course, above all there is love, which we have spoken about already.

There is one very severe element in the teaching of Jesus about personal life. It would be convenient to forget it, but it is there nevertheless, and we must attend to it. Jesus said, 'anyone who wants to follow me must deny himself and take up his cross and follow me'. Put like that it seems to contradict what we have just been saying; it sounds as if we ought to put ourselves out of the picture altogether. But Jesus said these hard things to his friends at the time when the crisis of his and their lives was approaching. He was, in fact, on the way to Jerusalem where he knew he would be put to death. So for us these words mean that there can come for us crises in which we have to put ourselves out of the picture, and devote everything we have and are, at whatever cost, to the cause which being a Christian involves for us at that time. This is what has happened to those who have been persecuted for their faith and to those who have gone to dangerous and difficult places for the sake of the Gospel. Crises of this sort can happen in any age, and to any Christian, and the words of Jesus are clear.

One of John Wesley's favourite teachings was that it was actually possible for a Christian in his life on earth to reach perfection in the love of God and of his neighbour; that is, by the power of the Spirit, really and truly to love God and his neighbour in the way described by Jesus without any imperfections whatever. Wesley even drew up a short list of those people of whom he believed this to be true. He did not put himself on the list. This probably seems very fanciful to us, especially as life and the choices we have to make have become so much more complicated since Wesley's time. Indeed he is probably wrong on this point. Yet there is an important truth behind Wesley's teaching on this matter. Christianity is not meant to be a half-and-half affair, but asks of us that we should set before ourselves nothing less than the highest possible standard, that is, the standard of perfect love. To be content with anything else than this quest is to fall below the teaching of the New Testament. We are so conscious of our imperfections that we shall always be reluctant to claim that we are making much progress, but unless we aim at the ideals set forth by Jesus we shall make no progress at all.

So we come round again to the point at which this chapter started—the many similarities between Christians and other people. These similarities are real; but we have discovered that under the similarities there are profound differences—differences in attitude to God and the world; different relationships to people, different objectives in life. And because these differences are bound to express themselves in action, a Christian is a different sort of person with a different style of life.

PART II

THE METHODIST APPROACH TO THIS COMMON CHRISTIAN FAITH

6

Why Methodism?

A VERY great deal of what has been said in this book so far is common ground for Christians of all denominations. Except for small groups of Christians who insist that to be a Christian you must believe that every word in the Bible is literally true, or that those baptised in infancy are not real members of the Church of Christ, nearly all Christians will probably accept the main lines of what has been said, with perhaps some reservations here and there.

Besides, those who disagree with parts of this book may be Methodists themselves, whereas those who accept those very same parts may be members of other Churches. In other words, the arguments which still go on about Christian teaching often do not follow denominational lines at all.

So it is high time to ask why there have to be separate denominations anyway. Why can we not drop the barriers and become one Church immediately? Part of the answer is that there are still unresolved differences of conviction between the Roman Catholic Church, the Orthodox Churches of Eastern Europe and the Churches which are neither Roman Catholic nor Orthodox. These include disagreements about the authority of the Pope, and about the priesthood, but are not nearly so numerous as people used to suppose. But they exist, and keep these Churches apart.

Yet so far as the non-Roman, non-Orthodox Churches are concerned, there is nowadays a wide-ranging consensus on the majority of important issues. In particular, the Church of England and the Methodist Church are very close. When the body called 'The Anglican–Methodist Unity Commission' drew up a scheme for the union of the two Churches, it concluded that there was enough agreement on matters of doctrine for the two Churches to become one, and although the scheme was rejected by the Church of England after being accepted by the Methodist Church, disagreement on doctrine was not the reason for the rejection, except in the minds of a few people. So why do the two Churches remain separate? Before we can answer this very good question we must go back into history, and discover how they became separate in the first place. This carries us back two hundred years or so, to the second half of the eighteenth century.

This period of British history is sometimes called the Age of Elegance, and sometimes the Age of Reason, and both names can be justified. Elegance there certainly was, in the dress and the manners and the literature of those who belonged to polite society in London, owned splendid and spacious houses in the country and went for a period each year to take the waters in Bath. Reason was certainly valued very highly, perhaps more highly than at any other time in British history, by those who discussed the deeper questions of human existence and behaviour in Edinburgh, Oxford, Cambridge and London, in frequent consultation with their fellow seekers-after-truth in Germany and France.

But there is another and darker side to the history

of the period. The people of elegance and reason formed a very small proportion of the population. Britain was an agricultural country in process of gradual transformation into an industrial country, though the process had not gone very far by the end of the eighteenth century. The people who worked on the land received very meagre wages, and their standard of living, as we should call it, was very low indeed, though many of those who lived in this way seem to have been content, perhaps because they believed that it was wrong to question the existing order. Those who migrated to the growing towns in search of work and wealth found themselves condemned to housing and to living conditions not greatly superior to those which are found on the edge of all the great cities of the Third World today. In London, in particular, the squalor and misery of the poor were plain for all to see within a very short distance of the comfortable houses of the rich and powerful. And it goes without saying that the peasants and the slum-dwellers had no say in the management of national or local affairs.

It is the business of the Church in every age to teach that every person is of equal value to God, and, as a consequence of this, to help in the building of a community in which the gap between rich and poor is diminished and members of all classes take a full part in the ordering of the nation's life. It is also the business of the Church to see that the message of the Gospel is brought home to people of all classes, including those whom social and other conditions have deprived of educational opportunities which are available only, as they were in eighteenth-century Britain, to the privileged few. Many Christians would now add—though this is a more controversial point—that it is the business of the Church to ally itself with the poor against the rich, when their interests clash, on the ground that the rich are very well able to look after themselves.

These propositions were not, of course, grasped or accepted by many in the period of which we speak; and the Church of England in the eighteenth century did not adequately fill any of the roles which are suggested above. This is a harsh statement to make, and there are many exceptions to it, in the shape of faithful parish clergymen, wise bishops and good-hearted members of the many Christian societies formed to help the under-privileged. Nevertheless there is much truth in it. The bishops were compelled to spend a period every year in the House of Lords, and, indeed, often owed their appointment to their party loyalty and had to vote for their party in the Lords; and many of their dioceses were so large that with the poor methods of travelling that were available they could not give any pastoral care to more than a few parishes. The country and small town clergy all too often ranged themselves with the local gentry to make sure that the 'peasants' 'knew their place', and kept it; the country people came to Church if they wanted to keep in with their masters, but the services and sermons rarely had anything to offer them. In the new industrial towns of the North and Midlands the population grew too rapidly for the clergy or the parish system to keep pace with their needs, and it was well into the nineteenth century before new parishes were formed in anything like adequate numbers.

There were, of course, other Christian groups, notably the Independents (whom we know better as Congregationalists), the Presbyterians, the Baptists and the Quakers, called indiscriminately Dissenters and Nonconformists by their contemporaries, though each group held very distinctive views. Their influence, however, though deep and lasting on their own members, was never widespread.

It was on this scene, with its alarming social contrasts, and in an atmosphere of deadness and apathy so far as religion was concerned, that John Wesley made his appearance in the forties of the eighteenth century. By birth and training, he was on the upper side of the intellectual and social division which ran through the country. Financially, he was not so privileged by any means, for his father, a clergyman, was ill-paid and extravagant, and found it impossible to provide for his very large family without much borrowing and the generosity of rich friends. But John, as a clergyman's son, a student at Oxford, and in due course himself a clergyman and the Fellow of an Oxford College, ranked with the lesser aristocracy. He could, no doubt, have made a great name for himself within the small circle of the intelligentsia by works of scholarship.

But from the time he went to Oxford he was afflicted by a deep dissatisfaction with himself as a Christian. In Oxford he joined a group of rather over-pious young men who had received the mocking title of 'the Methodists'. 'Methodists' were people who carried method and discipline too far, in the opinion of their critics. These men met regularly for prayer and Bible study and religious discussion, and did various works of charity. When John joined them, his younger brother, Charles, was already a member. They were not very much like the later

Methodists, but it was among them that John and Charles for a time found help in their restless quest for 'holiness', that is, for thoroughgoing Christian living.

After this group broke up the two brothers came to the conclusion that by doing missionary work they would find what they were looking for, and agreed to cross the Atlantic to preach to the settlers and the Indians in the newly founded colony of Georgia, in the South East of North America. But they quarrelled with the settlers, and never preached to the Indians. The enterprise was not a success for either of them, and when they came back to England they had still not found the secret of holiness.

In the light of their experience we can now see that their mistake lay in supposing that they could become perfect Christians by making mighty moral efforts for the benefit of others, and that if they did this they could be sure of God's favour and forgiveness. They had to learn that this was to put the cart before the horse; that, in fact, we become better Christians as a result of knowing that God has forgiven us; and God does not forgive us because we are good Christians, but in spite of the fact that we are not.

This truth came to John Wesley in London on 24 May 1738 in a flash of insight. It was not altogether sudden, for he was greatly helped towards it by a German called Peter Böhler, who belonged to a persecuted German church called the Moravian Church, or the Church of the Brethren, and was staying in London before finding a permanent home in America. Wesley's 'conversion' made a decisive difference to everything he afterwards did and said.

He now saw and announced that God's forgiveness does not depend on our goodness or our good deeds, but on his grace and love, and that this grace and love are offered to everyone on earth, however bad or however good, who asks for it in repentance and trust.

This was not, of course, a new thing to say. It is the main burden of what Jesus said to the 'publicans and sinners' who crowded round him, and of Paul's Letter to the Romans. But it had been overlaid in Wesley's time by the emphasis on living a good life and carrying out the duties of a Churchman, and the still very common English notion that we have to earn the love of God by living a virtuous life and doing good.

Its immediate effect on John Wesley—and, at much the same time, on his brother Charles—was to divert him from an intense absorption in the state of his own soul to an overwhelming urge to make known to other people what he had discovered for himself. This was the dominant motive for his nationwide and lifelong mission.

But, unlike many converts, he did not reject his past, or, least of all, repudiate the search for holiness. On the contrary, having told his hearers that their first need was for God's forgiveness and that this was readily available, he went on to insist that those who are forgiven are required and enabled by God to show love in all their relationships, and to do so in the most practical ways. Thus he showed that holiness was not just concerned with religious duties, but was an affair of everyday life. The Methodists were to be assiduous in their attendance at worship and in receiving the Sacrament of Holy Communion, and, for good measure, if they were really serious in their Christianity, to meet together in small groups to help each other and learn from each other.

The effect of this teaching, conveyed by John's sermons and writings, and by the words and popular music of Charles' hymns, was startling. It was evident mostly in the centres of population, many of them rapidly growing, but also over wide areas of rural England. Bristol, London and Newcastle became thriving centres of the movement; in Cornwall, then more industrial than it is today, and the urban areas of the Midlands, large crowds assembled to hear the preachers, and in town after town, and village after village, Methodist 'societies' were formed.

At first, there was a great deal of emotionalism and over-excitement among the uneducated people whom John Wesley addressed—not surprisingly, in view of the long period of apathetic ignorance of Christianity which had gone before. Partly, but not wholly, as a result of this, there was fierce opposition, some of it honest, some of it merely malicious, on the part of the clergy and others who thought that John Wesley was giving the 'lower classes' an exaggerated view of their station in life, and fomenting sedition in Church and State. But both the excitement and the opposition gradually calmed down, and many years before the end of his long life John Wesley was widely recognised as a great man, and a benefactor to his country, though many people still disapproved of his teachings and his methods.

He has his modern critics, of course, just as he had his contemporary opponents. What good is done, some of them ask, by constantly riding up and down the country, addressing large meetings at one place after another, perhaps impressing many people for the time being, and then leaving his converts high and dry to sort out their problems if they can? The answer is: very little, but John Wesley did not actually behave in this way. He certainly rode up and down the country—his record of miles on horseback has rarely, if ever, been broken—, but wherever people accepted his message, asked for God's forgiveness and resolved to lead a new life in the power of Christ, he organised them into a local society, appointed responsible men and women as their leaders and counsellors, and made sure to visit them again on his journeys from time to time.

A more substantial criticism is of the content of his preaching. It is said that he described the pains of hell which awaited unbelievers so colourfully that thousands of them hurriedly repented in order to avoid a dreadful fate. So they were brought into the Kingdom of God by sheer terror, and this is not a method or a motive of which a Christian can approve. Wesley certainly believed in hell-fire, like all other Christians of his day. But those who take the trouble to read all through the sermons which he preached will discover that he mentions it only occasionally, and very rarely indeed uses the prospect of it as a means of persuading his hearers. On nearly all occasions the dominant note of his appeal to sinners is emphasis on the universal and undeserved love of God, who wishes all men to be forgiven.

The criticism of Wesley's message which would be most serious, if it were justified, for people of our time, is this: in a time when the poor lived in misery, and the number of the poor was growing by leaps and bounds, and justice demanded that an acknowledged leader like John Wesley should lead them in a passionate campaign for social justice, he simply told them that they must put up patiently with their intolerable situation, since when they reached heaven they would have ample compensation. He did sometimes speak of the joys of heaven, and why not? And there is evidence that some of his followers understood him to mean that these were so wonderful that what happened in this life was of small importance. This was a natural misunderstanding in the minds of those whose hours of work were long and underpaid, whose housing was squalid and who had no means of seeking redress.

But Wesley was not responsible for the misunderstanding. He spent an immense amount of his time and energy trying to deal with the physical and mental needs of the underprivileged, setting up dispensaries, writing about medicines available to the poor, organising relief for the oppressed, opposing slavery, and, above all, founding schools. He was certainly not content with leaving people in physical misery while feeding them with promises of heaven. But why did he not start the revolution which was needed in this country to change the conditions under which the poor lived? He did not favour the idea of violent change. In politics he was in the centre or on the right, and what he saw happening in America, and, just before his death, in France, did not move him to change his mind. But he did believe that every single person was of equal value in the sight of God and therefore had a right to freedom and the opportunity for full personal development, and he made it his life-work to make available to every single person he could touch this good news and the means of bringing it into operation. So the Methodists of his day were not revolutionaries, but they were individual people with self-respect and human dignity, able to express themselves in words and actions and make responsible choices, and, in many cases to exercise leadership, whereas, without his preaching, these same people would have been downtrodden and abject.

Indeed, the effect of his work *was* revolutionary, though not in the commonly received sense; he helped to create a body of people who, with others in the half-century that followed his death, by activity in local and national politics, trade unionism, literature and education, did much to formulate and further the British version of democracy. The pity is that some, perhaps the majority, of Methodists in the same period never grasped the full implications of his Gospel, and much preferred the 'conservative' to the 'radical' elements in his thought.

Wesley did not achieve what he did achieve without setting up and maintaining a tightly knit organisation. All authority in the Methodist movement stemmed directly from him, and he made himself responsible for choosing, training and placing his helpers. A few of these were ordained clergymen, but for the most part they were not. The clergymen who sympathised with Wesley gave their support in the parishes where they served. They did not join the ranks of his 'travelling' or 'local' preachers. The 'travelling' preachers were those who gave up their ordinary occupation, and placed themselves at Wesley's disposal, acting as his 'assistants' in whatever area of the country he wanted them to be. They did not normally stay in one area for more than two years, and often for only one, but during that period they supervised all the Methodist societies to be found there. But they could not preach at all the services in every town and village, and Wesley appointed men and women who continued to live in their homes to do this. Hence the title 'local preachers'—the term which is still used of the lay preachers of the Methodist Church.

Every year Wesley summoned a select body of his friends and assistants to what he called 'the conference', often in Bristol, Leeds and Newcastle, often in London, and sometimes elsewhere. He listened to their advice, and made the decisions himself. But when he knew that he could not live much longer, in 1784 he chose a hundred of his travelling preachers to form the body which would legally take over his authority at his death, that is, direct and 'station' the preachers, and settle the policy of the Methodist Societies in the whole of Britain. The body which orders the affairs of the Methodist Church today is still called 'the Conference', and someone is elected each year to preside over it, in succession to Wesley.

It is clear that Wesley wished his movement to continue after his death, but he was in no sense setting up a rival institution to the Church of England. On the contrary, he expected all Methodists to be loyal members of the Church of England, and the Methodist Societies simply formed a community of those who followed the Methodist way of life, within the very loose framework of that Church.

But things did not turn out as he expected and hoped. In many places there was bad blood between the Anglicans and the Methodists. The Anglicans resented what they took to be interference with the ordinary work of the Church. The Methodists tended to believe that they were the only true Christians in the neighbourhood. The Methodists did not always wish to obey Wesley's instructions and receive Communion at the Parish Church. The parish clergy did not always welcome them. So the Methodists began to ask for communion from their own preachers.

Wesley closed his ears to any talk of this, or of separation, but in the end he himself took the step which made separation inevitable. He held that the Church of England was the best ordered Church in Christendom, but he did not believe that all its rules were of divine origin. It was a matter of rule— as it still is—that only bishops can ordain people to be ministers. Wesley decided, quite early in his life, that the Bible did not lay this down, but also allowed ministers to ordain others to be ministers. But for many years he refrained from ordaining any of his preachers, as he was not a bishop, in order not to disturb the peace of the Church of England. But in his later years he changed his mind. After the American War of Independence practically all the English clergymen who were in America came back to this country. Wesley had sent some of his preachers to America some years before, but they were not allowed to give Communion as they were not ordained. These men, being more acceptable to the Americans than the Anglican clergymen, stayed on after the war. So the situation was—no clergymen, many Methodist preachers and no sacraments for the Methodist people. Wesley at last acted. He ordained three men, one of them to be a Superintendent and to ordain others, and sent them across the Atlantic.

By this action Wesley set up the Methodist Church of America, by now far the largest Methodist Church in the world. But he also plainly broke the rules of the Church of England. He did not admit this, and actually ordained further people for work in Scotland and England. He claimed, sincerely, to live and die a member of the Church of England, and he was certainly never expelled. But when he died in 1791 the separation was unavoidable, and since 1795, by decision of the Methodist Conference, the Church of England and the Methodist Church have been two separate Churches.

7

The Methodist Contribution

THE LAST chapter should have made it clear why
and how the division between the Church of England and the Methodist Church came about. It may
well be that a greater degree of statesmanship on
each side could have prevented the break; certainly
both Anglicans and Methodists, or at least the great
majority of both, wish that it had never happened.

Why, then, does the division remain? For its part,
the Methodist Church is now resolved to heal the
breach. This was not always so. In fact, its own early
history produced divisions within its own ranks.
Smaller Methodist Churches, such as the Methodist
New Connexion, the Bible Christians and the
Primitive Methodists, appeared within thirty years
of Wesley's death by separating from the main body.
Each of these rebelled because they thought that the
old spirit of Methodism was being lost. And in the
middle of the nineteenth century there was a catastrophic division—catastrophic both in size and dis-
ruptive effect—due partly to arrogance in the parent
body (the Wesleyans), and partly to the bitter rejection of established authority in those who broke
away to form the United Methodist Free Church.

In the twentieth century the trend was completely
reversed. Early on, the number of Methodist
Churches was reduced to three—the Wesleyan

Methodists, the United Methodists and the Primitive Methodists, and in 1932 these three were united to form the Methodist Church. From that time forward Methodists turned their thoughts to reunion with the Church of England, and with the other Free Churches. There had always been Wesleyan Methodists who hoped for reunion, and only during a dark period of controversy during the nineteenth century was that hope damped. For the last forty years, under the impetus of the Ecumenical Movement, reunion with the Church of England has been actively discussed and planned.

A long period of conversations and negotiations reached its climax in 1969, when a scheme of union was put before both Churches. The Methodist Church accepted it by a commanding majority; the Church of England, no doubt because of some elements in the scheme which displeased many Anglicans, could not muster a large enough majority to be able to accept it. The same thing happened when the scheme was reintroduced in 1971. This gives us the reason why the Churches remain separate, at least for the time being.

Against its will, the Methodist Church remains separate and continues its own life. Wherever possible, it works closely with other Churches, and very many Anglicans, grieved by the rejection of the scheme of union, have entered wholeheartedly into local co-operation. Thankfully the issue of reunion is not dead, and discussions have been widened to include those Churches which did not take part in the previous negotiations. The Churches' Unity Commission has the task of looking fully into this matter. If a united Church emerges in the future, what contribution has Methodism to make to it? By asking this we shall also discover the distinctive qualities of Methodism which for the time being it must exercise in separation.

There are certain elements in the understanding and practice of the Christian faith, which, while not peculiar to Methodism, receive a special emphasis in Methodist life. This is not to say that they are to be found, or found in full measure, in every Methodist Church and Church member; but where Methodism is at its best, they are there.

The first is a double tradition of worship. Most Churches, it is fair to say, concentrate either on 'liturgical worship', that is, worship according to set forms; or on spontaneous worship, that is, worship which, in theory at least, arises from the needs and inspiration of the moment. On the whole, Churches which share in the 'Catholic' tradition—Roman Catholics, Orthodox and Anglican—have preferred liturgy; the Free Churches of Britain and America and other English-speaking countries, along with Presbyterian (or 'Reformed') Christians, have preferred spontaneity. In recent times, when it has been realised that much liturgical worship has become merely formal, and much so-called spontaneous worship tedious and repetitive, there has been a drawing-together of people from various traditions whose prime concern has been the renewing of worship in the whole Church. This has led to the breakdown of many barriers between the Churches.

Methodists who are most in accord with the principles of John Wesley have always been accustomed to the use of liturgies from the Anglican Book of Common Prayer, especially Mattins and Holy Communion, and have from time to time produced other liturgies closely allied to them. The

Covenant Service, which from Wesley's time has enabled each Methodist every year to renew his vows of Christian allegiance, has been passed on down the years with little alteration of its central liturgical core.

But most Methodist services on a Sunday morning or evening are not of this type. They claim to be free from a set pattern, and they include extemporary prayers, and lessons from Scripture chosen by the preacher, whether he uses the recommended series of lessons or not. Everyone knows that many of these services have become little more than a string of hymn, prayer, hymn, lesson, hymn, prayer, etc.—a kind of multiple sandwich. They scarcely illustrate the Methodist quest for spontaneity!

In the last few years, as part of the world-wide movement for the renewal of worship, a great change has come over both parts of the Methodist tradition, though it has not yet spread throughout the Church. The liturgical services have been re-written, with the express purposes of bringing in what is good from the worship of the whole Church down the ages, of making the words and the actions of worship understandable by all and of inviting the active participation of everyone present. The result of this work is the 'Methodist Service Book', which also suggests ways in which non-liturgical worship can have more meaning.

At the same time there have been many experiments in free worship, some more successful than others, which have involved modern music and modern musical instruments, as well as bodily movement, together with songs and readings in the modern idiom, and the greatest possible activity by the congregation. These experimental services are very valuable, but only when they take place against the background of more traditional worship. In this context they are the modern expression of an important element in Methodist tradition. So Methodism has tried to hold together form and spontaneity in worship, instead of concentrating on one kind of worship to the exclusion of the other.

The second feature of Methodism which may have a special part to play in the life of a united Church is the emphasis which it has always placed on social concern. Following Wesley's fierce opposition to slavery, Methodists have always devoted much energy to the discovery, and if possible, elimination of social evils, especially those calculated to diminish human dignity and curtail human rights. Notable modern examples are sustained opposition to apartheid in South Africa and to the racist régime in Rhodesia, but the studies, pronouncements and activities of the Social Responsibility Division of the Church cover large areas of human life, personal and social. Some people complain that it passes judgement on too many matters. But this is a superficial criticism, and certainly the Methodist Church does not encourage its members to keep out of politics. There are Methodist MPs of all parties in the House of Commons; they would all claim to have been brought up in the Methodist tradition of concern for social justice.

The third feature is a particular way of understanding the universal scope of the Gospel. This, like so many other things, has its origin in Wesley's own time. Many of his first partners, including George Whitefield himself, who was the man who persuaded Wesley to preach in the open air, against all his prejudices and many of his convictions, believed in predestination. That is to say, they held that God had decided, before the beginning of time, who was to be saved and go to heaven, and who was to be damned and go to hell. Wesley fought this teaching tooth and nail, root and branch. He held that God's grace was offered to every single person, and that no one's fate was fixed in advance. Each person was free to accept or reject God's offer. So he preached with as much fervour to the down-and-outs and rejects of society, who on the 'predestination view' were almost certainly damned, as to respectable and religiously inclined people.

It was in this spirit that some of Wesley's preachers, while he was still alive, started to travel up and down the world in order to preach to the 'heathen' (as they were then called); and shortly after his death the Wesleyan Methodist Missionary Society was founded. It was as missionaries, of course, that the preachers went to the newly independent nation of America, and when the Methodist Episcopal Church there was securely founded, missionaries set out from America to a larger number of countries than British Methodists could reach.

At home in England the impulse to bring the Gospel to the poor of the industrial revolution weakened during the nineteenth century among Wesleyan Methodists, who by thrift and hard work had mostly graduated to the middle classes. But the smaller Methodist groups retained a contact with working-class people which was greater than that of any Christian body until the Salvation Army was founded in the 1860s. At the end of the century Wesleyan Methodist interest revived, and 'Central Halls' were built in many large cities to meet the spiritual and physical needs of the underprivileged.

This all came from the dogged belief that all men can know and receive the love of God. There is a tendency nowadays to suppose that social and economic forces mould people's characters so firmly that not even the Gospel or the power of God can change them. In spite of this, Methodism remains committed to the belief that human nature can be changed, and rejects the opposite belief just as vigorously, and on the same grounds, that Wesley rejected predestination.

The fourth feature which Methodism can contribute to a united Church concerns the place in the Church of those who are not ordained ministers. Most of Wesley's helpers were laymen, some of them from a very poor educational background. Wesley set them a course of training which brought out their natural gifts, and then he gave them large responsibilities. Some he appointed to be 'travelling preachers', and these 'travelling preachers' developed into the Methodist ministers of the years since Wesley's death. But the majority remained laypeople—local preachers and class-leaders and officials of the Church, men and women with various functions. So laypeople from the start have shared in the leading of worship, in pastoral care and in the administration of the Methodist Church. Even so the Wesleyan Methodist Church came in course of time to be minister-controlled, until the principle of lay-ministerial partnership reasserted itself in this century. It may be that too much of the Church's work is still left to the minister, or claimed by him, and sometimes there is tension at this point. All Christian Churches, in various degrees, now maintain that the Church does not consist primarily of ministers, with laypeople in a subordinate role, but of ministers and laypeople in equal partnership. But the Methodist Church, having experienced this partnership for so long, ought to be able to give other Churches the fruit of this experience.

The fifth feature is a kind of invisible asset, hard to describe or recognise. It is perhaps best thought of as an insistence on the personal nature of Christianity, in a special sense. It is not to be confused with individualism. The idea is not that each of us travels through life and finds his way to God separately from everyone else. It is rather that each of us is invited as a person into the Kingdom of God— into a personal relation with God and other Christians: that for me it must be *my* personal choice to enter or stay out. In baptism I am brought into the Church, become a member of it and am given the power of the Holy Spirit to make my membership real. But there comes a time when I must decide for myself whether I wish to take up all the benefits and responsibilities of my membership. And if I decide, by the prompting of the Holy Spirit, to do so, I am thereby accepting Christ as my personal Saviour and Lord. I do not do this alone, but in the company and with the help of those who are further advanced in their knowledge of Christ, and those who are seeking for truth and life as I am. And afterwards my faith and theirs is built up by further conversation and united prayer and worship.

This is the background of Wesley's teaching on 'conversion', 'assurance' and 'Christian fellowship' —as well as of the constant use of the first personal pronoun in Charles Wesley's hymns. Conversion in Wesley's mind was not necessarily a violent change from extreme wickedness to full trust in Christ, though this seems to have happened sometimes. Rather it is a turning away from selfishness to make one's own the forgiveness and other gifts of God, which have been offered and promised already in baptism; and this can be either a process or a single event. Wesley also taught that God the Holy Spirit frequently gives to Christians the personal 'assurance' of being forgiven—the advantage of being freed from doubt as to whether they really are the children of God. He did not promise this gift of God to every Christian, and he certainly did not deny the name of Christian to those who never had it. But he taught his followers to expect it, and to welcome it if it came, as a relief and comfort in times of distress and pain.

As he often remarked, the Bible knows nothing of a solitary Christian, and he had the gravest doubts as to whether anyone who cultivated his Christian life in isolation from his fellows would remain a Christian for long. He arranged for all Methodists to meet together weekly in groups of twelve under a leader, for Bible study and prayer, and for conversation about their faith and their experience of God. This was, for him, 'fellowship in the Holy Spirit'—sharing what the Holy Spirit gave to each and all.

This form of personal religion can go wrong. People can become arrogant because they are converted, or never strive to advance beyond the early stage in the Christian life that conversion is; they can become cocksure about their relationship with God, instead of being humbled by the gift of assurance. And 'fellowship' can turn inward, or become merely the superficial companionship of people with similar tastes. But Methodism would not be itself if, in spite of the dangers, it did not remain personal. It might slip from its profound conviction that each human being is of equal value to God, and is the object of God's personal love and mercy.

Methodists have no wish to boast about these features, still less to keep them to themselves. Rather they wish to share them with all Christians, perhaps in modified and improved forms. Meanwhile they wish to hold them in trust for the coming great Church of the future, and hope to have the support of all other Christians in their endeavour to do so.

There are also, certainly, some Methodist failings which need to be eliminated when the Methodist Church becomes part of a larger body, if not before —a certain casualness about worship, for instance— homeliness and informality carried sometimes to an extreme. Another example is the tendency to value moral behaviour above worship, prayer and hard thinking. This moralism has led to an undue preoccupation with the question of alcoholic drink, when there are social evils at least as great which demand as much or more attention. It can be defended as a sound Christian position, though certainly not the only sound one, to abstain from alcohol altogether, as a personal witness, in order not to encourage in others a habit which may lead to disaster. But it cannot rightly be laid on every Christian as a duty. The Methodist Church has tended to do this in the past. It does so no longer, but traces of the old lack of balance still remain.

Methodism has much to learn from other Christians, it is evident, as well as something, perhaps, to teach them. It holds that only in a united Church can the truths committed to each separate denomination be seen in their true context, and the errors to which each denomination has been prone be seen as such and removed.

PART III

ONE CHURCH FOR ONE WORLD

8

The Way To Unity

NEAR the end of the last chapter occurred the phrase
'the coming great Church'. By this was meant the
Church of the future, which will be seen to be the
one Church of Jesus Christ. But is it really coming?
If it is, it is doing so rather slowly! In every town
in Britain, and in a great number of villages, there
are at least two separate denominations, and often
many more. Many Christians think of themselves
first and foremost as Anglicans, or Methodists, or
Baptists, long before they think of themselves as
members of the one Church of Christ. There is
much talk of unity among Christians in these days,
certainly, but action rarely follows. After all the
talk of the last fifty years the denominations seem
to be as separate from each other as ever.

Meanwhile, the largest Church of all, the Roman
Catholic Church—as well as the Orthodox Churches
of Eastern Europe—remains unwilling to unite with
any other Church, and we can scarcely speak of 'one
Church of Jesus Christ' unless the Roman Catholic
Church and the Orthodox Churches are included in
it.

But the outlook for Christian unity is not so bleak
as it seems at first sight. Fifty years ago—which is a
long time for individual people, but not so long in
the history of a nation or the Church—the denomi-

nations in Britain were not only separate, but often fiercely competitive with one another, and always at odds with one another on many matters of teaching and practice. In those days you could often see— as you sometimes still can—churches of several denominations lined up close to each other in the same street, and at that time you could safely guess that they had very little to do with each other, except on such occasions as Armistice Day, and that each of them would be very angry if children from its Sunday School decided to go to another Sunday School instead. It was not even uncommon to find a chapel belonging to each of the three separate Methodist Churches in quite a small village—so that the three buildings seemed to glower at each other across the village street.

But a vast change has come over the whole scene in fifty years. There were people working for better things from the days before the First World War. In 1910 an assembly in Edinburgh of missionaries from all over the world, with some representatives of the churches overseas which were the products of missionary work, agreed that it was foolish for each of the British and American and European denominations to plant new and separate churches under denominational names in Asia and Africa, while professing to preach the same Gospel of Jesus Christ. They decided to work together from then on as far as possible. After World War I, in 1920, the bishops of the Anglican Churches throughout the world, meeting in Lambeth, issued an appeal for Christian unity to 'all Christian people', and suggested ways in which it could be brought into effect.

So there were leaders and members in every Church more than fifty years ago who were anxious to heal divisions and bring Christians together. In some countries they eventually succeeded. The three Methodist Churches became one Church in 1932. This was not so difficult to bring about as some later unions have been, since all three Churches owed allegiance to John Wesley. In 1925 the United Church of Canada had been formed, but the Anglican Church found itself unable to join in. Before the Second World War the Churches in South India were planning union, and in Britain many conferences were held to find the best way forward for this country.

The war suspended these activities, but only temporarily. In 1947 the Church of South India came into existence, and its birth was an inspiration and an example to all who cared for unity. The Church of North India followed 23 years later, and all over the world the movement towards unity has gained momentum. We hope to see several more united Churches in the next few years, for instance in Sri Lanka and Australia.

Progress in Britain has been slower than in many other countries, though even here the Congregational Church and the Presbyterian Church of England have recently united to form the United Reformed Church. The most important discussions that have so far taken place are perhaps those between the Church of England and the Methodist Church, the two largest non-Roman Catholic Churches. If they had succeeded they would surely have quickened the progress of unity in every country where there are Anglicans and Methodists.

They did not succeed. The Church of England, as we have seen, could not in the end accept the great changes that would have been involved. This failure to unite caused deep disappointment in both Churches, and has led many people to give up all hope of visible unity between the Church of England and the other churches for a long time to come.

But the unity movement is grounded in the plain teaching of the New Testament, that there is only one Church of Jesus Christ, and that therefore the existence of a divided Church is contrary to the will of God. So the movement goes on and must go on in this country as elsewhere. The Roman Catholic Church, the United Reformed Church and the Baptist Churches and other smaller churches have now joined in the discussions with Anglicans and Methodists, and, as we have seen, the 'Churches' Unity Commission' is seeking to find a basis of union.

All this had led to the creation and continuance of a quite different atmosphere from that in which older Christians were brought up. Almost without exception, Christians of all denominations are on friendly, non-competitive terms with each other, and work together as closely as their convictions allow, and this is sometimes very closely indeed. It is now possible, as once it was not, for Free Churchmen to take Communion freely in Anglican Churches, and many Anglicans are happy to receive Communion from Free Church ministers.

This growth in understanding, and the need for it, are especially to be seen in neighbourhoods where very few of the inhabitants have the slightest interest in the Christian faith. In such places it is ludicrous for Christians to insist on remaining separate and on keeping their own denominational ways intact when united action is urgently required. So there are many 'Areas of Ecumenical Experiment'—areas where the churches work together as one body of Christians, and some of the rules and customs of each church are modified. Moreover, many church buildings are shared, especially in new or fairly new housing estates.

The Church of Rome for a long time took almost no notice of the Ecumenical Movement. The old hostility and suspicion between Roman Catholics and Protestants persisted until the time of Pope John XXIII (1958–1963). Then in a quite remarkable way a new age began for the Roman Catholic Church, and therefore for all other Christians. There must have been many Roman Catholics who were waiting for a lead to be given, and this is just what Pope John did. Roman Catholics and Protestants began to see each other as fellow-Christians, all baptised in the name of Father, Son and Holy Spirit. So they began to learn from each other and trust each other. Roman Catholics are now to be found at all conferences between Christians of different denominations, taking an active part in the proceedings. Official talks are being held on a world scale and on a national scale between the Roman Catholic Church and the Churches of the Anglican Communion, and likewise between the Roman Catholic Church and the Methodist Churches—and there are many other similar events going on. It is unlikely that in anything like the near future there will be an actual union between the Roman Catholic Church and any other Church; but the talks have shown that when prejudice and fear have been banished there are many important things on which Roman Catholics and non-Roman Catholics agree, and many areas of human life where they can work happily together. But is there any real need for all Christians to be collected into one Church? There are bound to be differences in belief and practice among Christians, and, so long as they work harmoniously together, as they are mostly doing nowadays, is there anything badly wrong? Surely 'spiritual' unity is what we need?

Supporters of visible Christian unity recognise the need for diversity within the Church, and certainly do not wish all the differences between Christians to be ironed out. They work for unity, not uniformity; for one Church which will contain and embrace many differences, especially the particular contributions of wisdom and worship that each denomination can bring.

For them 'spiritual' unity needs visible expression. So they speak of organic unity, the kind of unity possessed by a living organism, such as a human body. A human body is visibly and outwardly one; it is also inwardly one, directed and controlled by the person whose body it is, while he is alive and in good health. The inward spiritual unity of the Church has to be expressed by its outward, visible form. The 'outward' unity of the Church is a sham unless it is inwardly and spiritually united.

It is easy and tempting to become impatient with the long-drawn-out process of bringing the Churches as Churches together. Everyone engaged in this operation feels like this sometimes. This impatience leads people to say that the Churches as organisations ought to be scrapped altogether, or left to decay; and that true Christians ought to form themselves into ginger-groups, made up regardless of anyone's denomination, and then go and spread Christian unity far and wide. This is a very attractive idea and its supporters have an enthusiasm which older people do not always have. And on the face of it, it would save millions of pounds and an immense amount of energy. But there is a difficulty. Human beings are so made that they have to organise themselves if they are going to get anything done. Even ecumenical ginger-groups have to have a committee and a secretary and money for expenses. So if we follow this idea, we shall have another set of organisations in addition to the Churches, and unity will be farther off than ever. So it is better for those who long for unity to stay inside their Churches, and work in ginger-groups from that position.

This becomes clearer still when we remember that Christian unity is not just a local or national affair, but a global one. For the achievement of unity all over the world there has to be an organisation which brings the Churches together on an international scale and can help to release the power of the Spirit in every country and neighbourhood. It is for this purpose that the World Council of Churches exists, and it has to be a Council of Churches, not of individual Christians, if it to to do its work. It has 279 member-Churches, not yet including the Roman Catholic Church. It was thought of before the Second World War, planned as the war went on, and brought into existence after it was over.

It has held five Assemblies so far, the last of them in Nairobi, Kenya, in 1975. It has a programme which is almost too big and complicated to grasp, from the careful study of Christian doctrine and the differences between the teachings of the various Churches to the organisation of relief for refugees all over the world.

When it was created, it was mostly made up of Churches from Europe, Britain and America. Now, most of the member-Churches are from Asia, Africa and Latin America; from the Third World, in fact. This means that the World Council has come to give great attention—not by any means too soon—to world poverty and the injustices inflicted by one race on another. The best known example of this is the 'Programme to Combat Racism', which involves the sending of money for education and social welfare to organisations which aim at overthrowing racist régimes.

The Programme has been much criticised, on the ground that money given for educational and social purposes may be spent on the purchase of arms for revolutionary action. In spite of criticism the World Council has continued the programme as the most practical way of helping to end the oppression of one race by another, and makes every effort to ensure that the money is not misused.

The Programme to Combat Racism is a very small part of the World Council's varied activity. All of it comes under the heading of 'Jesus Christ Frees and Unites', the slogan of the Fifth Assembly in 1975. The World Council of Churches is committed to the view, already expressed in this book, that the saving work of Christ embraces the whole of human life, personal and social, including the realms of politics and economics as well as what is usually called 'the spiritual side of life', and calls on the Churches to unite in confessing Christ as the World's Saviour in this all-embracing sense. Sometimes it may seem to emphasise politics too much; this false impression comes in part from the fact that the Press quotes its political pronouncements far more often than what it has to say on the inner life of Christians and Churches. There is little to be said for the view that the Church, or the Council of Churches, should keep out of politics. The Bible certainly does not say this.

The existence of the World Council of Churches is a living proof of the fact that the unity which Christians are seeking is not the unity of the Church alone. The unity of the Church is for the sake of the unity of mankind, a very distant goal, as it seems at the moment, yet the goal at which responsible people in every nation are aiming. The Church is in a poor position to urge the nations and races and classes of the world to unite with each other, while it remains divided within itself. There is very clear evidence of this in Northern Ireland, even though the causes of conflict there are not mainly religious. But if Christian people inside nations, and across the frontiers of nations, were able to reconcile their differences without abandoning their convictions, an example of peace would be provided for which at present people look in vain, and an influence for peace would be released into the world with consequences which it would be hard to overestimate.

This is a Bible teaching, for it is the argument of the Letter to the Ephesians. The author says that it was God's purpose 'that the universe, all in heaven and on earth, should be brought into a unity in Christ' (Ephesians 1.9, 10). To bring this about Christ came to redeem mankind and reconcile its warring factions, focused at that time in the division between Jews and Gentiles. Those who heard his message and received the forgiveness of their sins became members of his Body, the Church, of which he is the Head. This one Church, inspired by one Spirit, holding out one hope, and confessing one Lord, one faith, one baptism, and one God and Father of all, is to grow, and to go from strength to strength, till it includes all mankind. Thus the unity of the Church is to make possible, and, indeed, to make real, the unity of mankind. 'So we all at last attain to the unity inherent in our faith and our knowledge of the Son of God—to mature manhood, measured by nothing less than the full stature of Christ' (Ephesians 4.13).

Index